UNDERSTANDING
ALAN BENNETT

Understanding Contemporary British Literature
Matthew J. Bruccoli, Series Editor

UNDERSTANDING
Alan
BENNETT

Peter Wolfe

UNIVERSITY OF SOUTH CAROLINA PRESS

© 1999 University of South Carolina

Published in Columbia, South Carolina, by the
University of South Carolina Press

Manufactured in the United States of America

03   02   01   00   99   5   4   3   2   1

Library of Congress Cataloging-in-Publication Data

Wolfe, Peter, 1933–
    Understanding Alan Bennett / Peter Wolfe.
        p.   cm. — (Understanding contemporary British literature)
    Includes bibliographical references (p.) and index.

    ISBN 1-57003-280-7
    1. Bennett, Alan, 1934—Criticism and interpretation.   I. Title.
II. Series.
PR6052.E5 Z93   1999
822'.914—dc21   98-40227

With love, to Retta
for knowing when to walk away
from a dish of French toast

CONTENTS

EDITOR'S PREFACE

The volumes of *Understanding Contemporary British Literature* have been planned as guides or companions for students as well as good nonacademic readers. The editor and publisher perceive a need for these volumes because much of the influential contemporary literature makes special demands. Uninitiated readers encounter difficulty in approaching works that depart from the traditional forms and techniques of prose and poetry. Literature relies on conventions, but the conventions keep evolving; new writers form their own conventions—which in time may become familiar. Put simply, *UCBL* provides instruction in how to read certain contemporary writers—identifying and explicating their material, themes, use of language, point of view, structures, symbolism, and responses to experience.

The word *understanding* in the titles was deliberately chosen. Many willing readers lack an adequate understanding of how contemporary literature works; that is, what the author is attempting to express and the means by which it is conveyed. Although the criticism and analysis in the series have been aimed at a level of general accessibility, these introductory volumes are meant to be applied in conjunction with the works they cover. They do not provide a substitute for the works and authors they introduce, but rather prepare the reader for more profitable literary experiences.

M. J. B.

ACKNOWLEDGMENTS

The author and publisher join hands in thanking those whose time and energy went into the preparation of this book: Lawrence and Pat Barton, who supplied details pertaining to the North-of-England background of the Bennett scripts; Ruth Bohan, who shared with me her knowledge of art history; Brenda Jaeger, who typed and edited the final draft; Jane Williamson and Nitram Egas, who helped organize a grant that spend the book's completion. The combined help of the following people amounts to a major contribution: Robert Ainsworth, Paula Coalier, Eugene Hacker, Gloria Henderson, Bert Kimmel, Bruce Lowney, Ethan Robert, Evelyn Schwabe, Anne Taylor, Charles Walker, and Jules White.

PRODUCTION DATES

Beyond the Fringe
      22 August 1960, Cranston Street Hall, Edinburgh
Forty Years On
      31 October 1968, Apollo Theatre, London
Getting On
      14 October 1971, Queen's Theatre, London
A Day Out
      24 December 1972 on BBC-TV2
Habeas Corpus
      10 May 1973, Lyric Theatre, London
Sunset across the Bay
      20 February 1975 on BBC-TV
The Old Country
      7 September 1977, Queen's Theatre, London
A Visit from Miss Prothero
      11 January 1978 on BBC-TV
Me, I'm Afraid of Virginia Woolf
      2 December 1978 on London Weekend Television
Green Forms
      16 December 1978 on London Weekend Television
The Old Crowd
      27 January 1979 on London Weekend Television
Afternoon Off
      3 February 1979 on London Weekend Television
One Fine Day
      17 February 1979 on London Weekend Television
All Day on the Sands
      24 February 1979 on London Weekend Television
Enjoy
      15 October 1980, Vaudeville Theatre, London
Intensive Care
      9 November 1982 on BBC-TV

PRODUCTION DATES

Our Winnie
> 12 November 1982 on BBC-TV2

A Woman of No Importance
> 19 November 1982 on BBC-TV2

An Englishman Abroad
> 29 November 1982 on BBC-TV2;
> also 1 December 1988 (as part of the live production *Single Spies*)

Rolling Home
> 3 December 1982 on BBC-TV2

Marks
> 10 December 1982 on BBC-TV2

Say Something Happened
> 17 December 1982 on BBC-TV2

A Day Out
> 30 December 1982 on BBC-TV

A Private Function: A Screenplay
> 21 November 1984

The Insurance Man
> 23 February 1986 on BBC-TV2

Prick up Your Ears (A Screenplay)
> 14 July 1986

Kafka's Dick
> 23 September 1986, Royal Court Theatre, London

A Chip in the Sugar (from *Talking Heads*)
> 19 April 1988 on BBC-TV (as *The Middleaged Man*);
> also 11 June 1996, with *A Bed among the Lentils* and *Soldiering On* as *Talking Heads,* Minerva Theatre, Chichester

A Bed among the Lentils (from *Talking Heads*)
> 19 April 1988 on BBC-TV

PRODUCTION DATES

A Lady of Letters (from *Talking Heads*)
        19 April 1988 on BBC-TV (as *Miss Ruddock*)
Her Big Chance (from *Talking Heads*)
        19 April 1988 on BBC-TV (as *The Extra*)
Soldiering On (from *Talking Heads*)
        19 April 1988 on BBC-TV
A Cream Cracker under the Settee (from *Talking Heads*)
        19 April 1988 on BBC-TV (as *Doris*)
Single Spies (including *An Englishman Abroad* and *A Question of Attribution*)
        1 December 1988, Royal National Theatre, London
The Wind in the Willows
        14 December 1990, Royal National Theatre, London
Talking Heads
        6 February 1992, Comedy Theatre, London
The Madness of George III
        28 November 1991, Royal National Theatre, London
The Madness of King George
        Movie released 1994

CHAPTER ONE

Tracking the Fringe

Playwright Alan Bennett was both born (in 1934) and brought up in the industrial town of Leeds. Even as a child, this butcher's son disclosed an early interest in culture, attending weekly concerts by the Yorkshire Symphony Orchestra and thinking a good deal about religion. This flair has persisted. He has used music in several of his plays, and in 1988 he said that he never outgrew his religious upbringing,[1] a truth conveyed by both the recurrence of clergymen in his work and his having written, as recently as 1997, a television series based on the New Testament.[2] But before he could think seriously about a career in the vicarage or elsewhere, he first had to do his national service. Thus he took infantry training and then studied Russian, first at Coulsdon and then at Cambridge, through the Joint Services Language Course. His 1953 Cambridge stint also helped him decide to which of England's two great universities he would apply. His outstanding scholastic record won him acceptance of Exeter College, Oxford, from which he graduated with a first-class degree in 1955. He remained an Oxonian until 1962, teaching medieval history at Magdalen College while researching a Ph.D. dissertation (never finished) on the retinue of England's Richard II between 1388 and 1399.

Other interests overrode history. Discovering in himself the ability to make people laugh, he did stand-up comedy routines at Exeter's Junior Common Room. These turns won him celebrity as a cabaret performer throughout the university. His celebrity grew. In August 1960, he and three other men who never planned to have show business careers launched a revue at Edinburgh's Lyceum Theatre, which comprised skits, parodies, songs, and monologues on subjects including nuclear holocaust, the cold war, and capital punishment. Appearing nightly at 10:45 on the bare stage of Edinburgh's Cranston Street Hall dressed in suits and dark sweaters,[3] Oxonians Bennett and Dudley Moore (b. 1935) together with Cambridge men Jonathan Miller (b. 1934) and Peter Cook (1937–95)[4] revitalized British stage comedy. The Edinburgh Festival had been including in its annual summer program concerts and plays that attracted audiences from all over Great Britain. Then, as Roger Wilmut has explained, the festival, spotting the chance for an artistic breakthrough, expanded its format: "From the mid-fifties onward this annual feast of music and drama had the added attraction of unofficial performances by various small and often experimental theatre and review groups . . . the 'Fringe' of the Festival."[5] In 1960, the festival's director, John Bassett, proposed another addition—the revue called *Beyond the Fringe* (BTF). The rest is history, laughter, or a chapter in the history of stage comedy. BTF went to London's Fortune Theatre the following May, where it ran for more than a year before moving to New York's John Golden Theatre for a two-year run starting in October 1962.

I

Like the members of the Auden Group in the 1930s and England's Angry Young Men two decades later, the foursome comprising BTF split up to pursue their own careers by the time they reached the age of thirty. Peter Cook became a London nightclub entertainer and impresario; Dr. Jonathan Miller returned full time to medicine; Dudley Moore won praise as a jazz pianist, screen actor, and offbeat humorist. The remaining member of the quartet, Alan Bennett, had the most dubious professional outlook when the group folded, an impression he might have encouraged with his reticence and self-deprecating manner. Bennett defies all standard formulas for show-business success. In 1991, Jack Kroll called him "the least famous of the four," and, following suit, Ben Brantley said in 1995 that Bennett "was certainly the quietest and most cryptic of the quartet."[6] Nicholas de Jongh, writing in 1988, referred to his "relatively modest expectations."[7] But de Jongh also pointed out that Bennett had already outstripped these hopes. His success fuses talent, hard work, and love for his craft. That craft he defines broadly. Like Noël Coward and John Osborne before him, he has made the theater his turf, having worked as an actor, a director, a playwright, a lyricist, a set designer, a costumer, a make-up artist, and a lighting technician. And, as self-effacing as he seems, this theatrical genius who grew up in a working-class Leeds family "seems to be everywhere," claimed Matt Wolf in the *Times* of London.[8] Wolf's "everywhere" only overstates the case modestly. In January 1992, when Wolf was writing, Bennett had two plays running in London's West End; he had recently acted in one of his own telescripts; and his suite of monologues, *Talking Heads,* written originally for television, was opening in London's Comedy Theatre.

This success was no fluke. The years have confirmed Bennett's theatrical eminence. The casts of his plays, starting with *Forty Years On* in 1968, have included luminaries like John Gielgud, Alec Guinness, Joan Plowright, Maggie Smith, Alan Bates, and Daniel Day Lewis. *Talking Heads* went through twenty-seven printings between its original 1988 publication date and 1995. *Single Spies* won the Olivier Award as England's best comedy for 1988; Bennett, moreover, acted in both of the plays included in this double bill, and he directed one of them. His prominence extends to the cinema. Along with Helen Mirren and Nigel Hawthorne, the film's two leading players, he was nominated for an Academy Award for writing *The Madness of King George* (1994), in which he also acted a small role. Even away from the performing arts, he has won honors. He contributes regularly to the *London Review of Books,* and his 1994 book of memoirs, *Writing Home,* rose to the top of England's bestseller list. Other writers as well as readers and actors admire him. Michael Ratcliffe calls him "one of the funniest and most fastidious writers working in England today"; Brantley believes that, along with Tom Stoppard, he's the "slyest . . . and most elegant of contemporary British dramatists"; eschewing comparisons, David Nokes, writing in the *TLS,* says he's "probably our greatest living dramatist."[9]

This acclaim runs afoul of his persona. Wry and reticent, Bennett has always shunned the spotlight, going as far as declining a dinner invitation to the Kennedy White House. Laurence Olivier and Richard Burton both draw the fire of this "self-effacing giant of the English stage" for having adopted "the sudden fortissimos, the instant access to emotion, and all the characteristics of the shouting school of acting."[10] Bennett's scorn for the florid and the overdone shows in his stagecraft. Like

Chekhov, he aims, in his work, for a smooth, even texture rather than a series of dramatic crescendos. Action for its own sake means little to him. Many of his characters occupy themselves with maintaining a facade, fighting boredom, and filling up idle hours. Guy Burgess, an English spy, appears in *An Englishman Abroad* (1988) some seven years after his defection to the USSR—that is, at a time when he has ceased being a news item in either London or Moscow. The Regency Crisis depicted in *Madness* inhibits dramatic drive. The king's derangement brings matters of state to a halt; no courtier dares risk his political future on an imponderable like the royal sanity. Nor can George himself advance events while delusional.

The stalemate that causes other government functionaries to wait for George's condition to change evokes Chekhov again, allowing people to be themselves rather than serving a plot. But while Bennett certainly does follow Chekhov in his avoidance of clearly defined beginnings, middles, and ends, his works lack the waywardness he imputed to them in 1979 when he said, "they wander, they joke, and they don't reach too many conclusions."[11] The fluidity of structure he is hinting at internalizes dramatic action and idea, developing them on the inner planes of perceptions. Subtext—that is, the difference between what is said and what is thought—claims more and more of the playgoer's attention. *The Madness of George III* (1991), the monologue *A Chip in the Sugar* (1987), and the 1984 screenplay *A Private Function* all end with a restoration of the status quo; in fact, someone says at the end of *Function,* "the status quo has been restored."[12] But, because each coin in Bennett has at least two sides, his spokesman for returning to the status quo has omitted something vital. Developments in all three works have forced him and the other characters to rethink the realities they live by, assess them, and resolve to live them through at a heightened, usually more painful, level of awareness. That most of Bennett's people face such challenges bravely creates some key tensions, one of which Harold Hobson noted in 1981: "Mr. Bennett has a strange and valuable talent for combining the affectionate with the uncomfortable."[13]

This combination begets an unforced rhythm of mood that creates meaning for Bennett at several dramatic levels. Thus in 1990 he adapted with great box-office success Kenneth Grahame's *Wind in the Willows* (1908), a children's story with adult themes. The adaptation benefited from Bennett's knack for spotting something vital out of the corner of his eye, often the way the fantastic permeates the everyday. What he admired in both the poet W. H. Auden and the film director Alfred Hitchcock in 1990 applies just as strictly to himself: "Auden is good at casting a spell, hinting at horrors just around the corner, and he uses Hitchcock's technique of investing the ordinary and the domestic with nightmare and suspense."[14] Setting in both the television drama *The Old Crowd* (1979) and the stage play *Enjoy* (1980) mingles the homey and the horrific. *Enjoy* unfolds in a rusty, dilapidated back-to-back, or row house, the last of its kind to survive in a working-class neighborhood in Leeds slated for demolition as part of an urban renewal plan.

More coziness follows, again with a stinger in its tail. The action is developed mostly by a retired couple, their two grown children, and a grandson. But this scenario builds a false sense of security that Bennett overturns. In fact, his greatest shock comes near the end, in the revelation that the ugliness he has been describing stems from a nuclear family. No bulwark against cruelty, the tatty, rundown Craven home has been unleashing for years the horrors that have turned the younger generation into monsters. *The Old Crowd* also wheels in the orbit of the family—this time, one from the privileged class. With Lindsay Anderson's sure-handed direction either mitigating or mocking the uncoiling devastation, the relatives and close friends comprising the old crowd of the play's title rival their hirelings in wickedness.

Bennett has explained this wildness. His introduction to *Talking Heads* ends with the words "life is generally something that happens elsewhere" (*TH* 13). Sensitive to the dynamism of the echoes put out by absent things, Bennett quotes E. M. Forster in his diary for January 1987: "Only what is seen sideways sinks deep" (*WH* 154). In the same vein, he quotes Madame de Sévigné on the subject of sightseeing: "What I see tires me and what I don't see worries me" (*WH* 155). These diary entries lend weight to Donald Lyons's 1992 statement, "Bennett's talent is that of a miniaturist—epyllion rather than epic."[15] Not only do the scaled-down and the muted tally with his reticence; as is seen in his admiration of Auden and Hitchcock, his attraction to cameo portraiture, as opposed to the heroic and grand, also gives him access to the unrevealed and the surmised. Attuned to the rhythms underlying the daily plod of life, he discusses Mr. Toad of *The Wind in the Willows* as one whose abrasiveness has made him an outsider despite his money. Bennett adds that the social adjustment and acceptance eluding Mr. Toad often hinge on an ability to "keep it under" (*WH* 224)—that is, to rein in traits offensive to others, like ostentation and loudness.

Thus a Bennett play can deal just as vitally with the unseen—those impulses and drives people suppress to survive socially—as with the overt. Sometimes, as in *Enjoy* and *Soldiering On* (1987), from *Talking Heads,* this covertness has roots in the distant past and refers to hidden family guilt. In *An Englishman Abroad,* stealth is a goal in itself. To assert his uniqueness, Guy Burgess drifts into espionage. His passing on highly classified secrets to the Soviets hones his sense of self; he gloats over his colleagues' ignorance of his activities. But sometimes the self in Bennett seeks closure with others rather than separation; the stresses of daily living can create the need to seek comfort in the group. One source of stress is the pawn complex fostered by holding one's own in a competitive society. If Bennett's people agree with their creator that what counts in life usually happens at a distance from the perceiver, then a sense of personal inferiority oscillates in the canon with a sense of consequence looming beyond the depicted action. Many of Bennett's characters worry about their ineffectuality. In *Me, I'm Afraid of Virginia Woolf* (London Weekend Television, December 1978), a thirty-five-year-old English teacher named Trevor Hopkins always carries a book, the reading of which distracts him from the disapproving or threatening looks he imagines are directed at him by strangers. His good job and robust health notwithstanding, this English Midlands version of a Woody Allen figure suffers from an angst familiar to many others in the Bennett canon.

Hopkins's ability to function despite feeling badgered by others calls for an acting technique resilient and adaptive enough to capture without distorting both his social and psychic cramp. It also bespeaks in Bennett himself a doubleness that Stephen Schiff, writing in 1993, put at the heart of his comic vision: "There is a duality that runs through Bennett and through his work: an awareness that whatever we pretend to be on the outside is a deception; that underneath we are all weak, noisome, and . . . deeply embarrassing."[16] This duality brings Bennett's plays closer to real life. His comedy isn't preemptive. As early as 1960, he understood that, just as any life has both its rewards and regrets, so can a play or film provoke both laughter and tears. This insight has improved his writing. The title of his 1971 play *Getting On* hints at the importance of retaining cheer and goodwill while slogging through life's ordeals. Bennett's BTF monologue "The English Way of Death" also tried to refresh its audience's moral outlooks by fusing sorrow and fun.[17] His first full-length play, *Forty Years On* (1968), which he has called "part play, part revue" (*BTF* 156), is nostalgic and astringent, elegiac and unsettling.

This Janus-like work even parodies itself. Of the play within a play about to be performed, the main character says, "What we are to see is neither comedy nor tragedy, but a mixture of both."[18] His addressing the audience directly imparts an ironic foreshadowing to the interior play, inviting both parallels and contrasts with the main action. The mixed form of *Forty Years On* affords Bennett both access to and distance from his theme. His self-knowledge expands. Chekhov-like, he approves the passing of the obsolete English codes and norms he knows he will miss because their passing evokes his lost youth. Sense tugs against sensibility. Though the ways of Granny's generation must be sacrificed to social progress, their going leaves one sad and empty. The moment is one of sweet sorrow. *Enjoy* deals with the same ambiguity. The old-world coziness and charm that stir feelings of nostalgia in this play rest on a foundation of backwardness, problems in health care, and economic injustice.

II

Bennett's bittersweet comedy has caused problems in production. Speaking of his lead actor in *Getting On,* he said, "Kenneth More saw the piece as a comedy while I was trying to keep it a serious play" (*One* 14). Yet the Socialist member of Parliament More played grew up with a duality that still touches him, as he explains to a television interviewer: "I am a product of the State System and admirable though it may be in some respects in others it is appalling" (*One* 159). Can the breach be repaired? Perhaps duality defines life for Bennett just as evolution did for Darwin or the tragic operation of the will did for Schopenhauer. Speaking in 1996 of the tendency of royalty both to be on a level with commoners and to demand their subordination, Bennett notes, "Like the rest of us I suppose they just want things both ways."[19]

Our century's avatar of self-division for Bennett and the inspiration for two of his plays is Franz Kafka (1883–1924). Having spoken of Kafka's desire to be "somebody and nobody at the same time" (*WH* 147), Bennett portrays the dying Czech author in *Kafka's Dick* (1986) as coveting both obscurity and fame. Kafka ordered his friend and literary executor Max Brod both to burn all Kafka's manuscripts and to dissuade all would-be biographers from probing his life. Yet he would also have resented the neglect had Brod followed orders. Kafka's job as a minor executive in Prague's Workers Accident Insurance Insti-tute fueled his doubleness. "To be deprived was to be endowed," said Bennett of those seeking compensation for work-related injuries (*WH* 359). Whereas the maimed and the mutilated en-joy a good chance for compensation, the whole and the healthy slouch home in empty-handed frustration. The 1987 essay "Kafka in Las Vegas" also calls Kafka both mourner and executioner (*WH* 336). Bennett is no doubt referring to Kafka's largeness of spirit. But, mindful of this man's crotchets and foibles, he is also wondering if the mystical self-detachment that gave Kafka in-sight into both sides of an issue did not owe something to inde-cisiveness, too. Was his all-encompassing sympathy a maneuver cooked up to hide his reluctance to take a stand? Bennett's de-scription of Kafka inhabiting garrets, burrows, and cubbyholes (*WH* 341) conjures up the image of a man ducking the responsi-bility of choice. The enclosure that offers protection from in-truders also blocks the healthy flow of air and light.

The frequency with which Bennett's imagination seeks out Kafka is instructive. Besides having written two full-length plays about the Czech author, *Writing Home* includes twenty-two ref-erences to him, some of which appear in discussions of other writers. For example, after referring to the poet Philip Larkin "wanting his cake but not wanting to be thought he enjoys eat-ing it" (*WH* 369), Bennett says that among writers, Larkin "most resembles" Kafka (*WH* 374). This judgment recalls Graham Greene's labeling Dickens a Manichean and citing Henry James's alleged Judas complex. Though supported by evidence, Bennett's commentary of Larkin turns the reader's attention back to Bennett himself. Again, evidence comes forth to keep it there. Now Bennett is always sharply aware of physical setting; underlying *An Englishman Abroad,* for instance, is the contrast between London chic and Moscow drabness (*WH* 210). The contrast is typical. Though a historian by training, Bennett has thought just as deeply about geographical differences as about temporal ones. The laws invoked by place started making inroads on his psyche in his late teens, when he began studying Russian at Cambridge as part of his national service. He found himself torn between the emotional demands created by his northern provincial roots and the elegance he had come to equate with London, the Oxbridge circuit, and BBC English ("speaking properly"). The Kulturkampf had taken root when his mother told him, some years earlier (*WH* ix–x), that she once met T. S. Eliot. Eliot married a Leeds girl, Valerie Fletcher, whose parents were customers of Walter Bennett, Alan's butcher father. As a boy, Alan delivered meat to Eliot's future mother-in-law.

Since making the connection between his childhood home and Valerie Eliot's, he has always felt pulled by the conflicting claims of his native North and the genteel South. The tension pits the innate against the acquired, the rough against the polished, nature against culture, and the mill and the mine against the cosmopolitan glitter of Mayfair and the West End. The privilege he equates with London and the south counties inspires him; as J. B. Miller notes, Bennett writes convincingly about royalty and the haute bourgeois world of art.[20] Bennett has also lived in London for most of his adulthood, having made the place the focus of both his social and professional lives.

Conversely, he has retained strong emotional bonds with the Leeds childhood that centered on his father's shop. "Truly, the North is another country, where they do things differently," said David Starkey in 1996.[21] Bennett has been conveying this uniqueness with great relish since his first television plays, *A Day Out* (1972) and *Sunset across the Bay* (1975). Though *Enjoy* remains his only stage play set in the North, the six television monologues comprising *Talking Heads,* the film *A Private Function,* and all but one of the telescripts making up *Objects of Affection* (1982) have a northern setting, as do three of the five telescripts collected as *The Writer in Disguise* (1985). Finally, the 1991 essay "Leeds Trams" (*WH* 11–14) recovers with deep affection the upholstery, the route numbers, and the routines of the conductors and ticket inspectors in charge of the trams he rode as a boy. Both here and elsewhere, he conveys the smell, touch, taste, and feel of the North, teasing out a "moral dimension" (*WH* 14) lacking in England's more comfortable South. In the plays, particularly, he evokes the local northern flavor without cataloging local details. But local details spring to mind anyway, because they are displayed with such artistry. The dismal red brick row houses of Leeds, with their worn, faded curtains, discolored mirrors, and dresser drawers stuffed with postcards from bygone seaside holidays continue to fire Bennett's imagination.

And so does northern speech. Bennett has both the pitch and the ear to simulate the Leeds dialect without descending to caricature. Like those earlier men from the North, both of whom wrote plays, Arnold Bennett (no relation) and D. H. Lawrence, he avoids giving the impression of explaining the actions of provincial clods to an audience of fellow sophisticates. He would rather let those provincials surprise—and delight—him. But besides standing on equal ground with them, he can also individualize them within a roughly uniform speech pattern. Sometimes personality is a function of selection. In his 4 January 1996 "Diary," published in the *London Review of Books,* he tells how female characters spoke most of the lines in the Leeds-based *Enjoy* but how men do most of the talking in the works set in London.[22] Social class and educational level also influence speech in Bennett, often in an original way; as the television plays *All Day on the Sands* (1979) and *Marks* (1982) show, voices and vocabularies often indicate, with obvious giveaways, what the speakers want to be rather than what they are: for example, an elderly working-class couple in *Sands* affects highborn speech to impress others and nearly gets it right. Then there are the topics the characters discuss, a motif noted by John Wilmut: "Most of [Bennett's] writing . . . centres on the north of England, which accounts for his preoccupation with subjects not normally considered funny, such as funerals and illness."[23] Wilmut is right. *Enjoy, Getting On,* and the video script *A Cream Cracker under the Settee* (1987) all include the infirm and the dying. Characters do die in *The Old Crowd, Rolling Home* (1982), and *Intensive Care* (1982). And, as Bennett himself points out in the Introduction to *Objects of Affection,* three of the scripts in the book unfold in a hospital, one in a cemetery, and one other in both places.[24]

Irony steers this grimness away from self-pity or heavy-handed moralizing. Irony also sorts well with Bennett's vision of England as a place that's small, class ridden, and excessively ironic to begin with. This excessiveness, he knows, can cause pain when overdone. If it makes for charm, it also blocks vigor, generosity, and insight into larger moral issues. Guy Burgess, the treasonous ex-diplomat of *An Englishman Abroad,* is said to have "bags of charm" (*OA* 228). The claim sounds valid; he is, after all, one of the eponyms referred to in *Objects of Affection,* the anthology in which *Englishman* appears. Yet the secrets he handed to the Soviets may have sent hundreds of his country-men to torture and death, and at the time of the play he is so sodden with booze that his Soviet hosts assign only apprentice spies to watch him. The actress Coral Browne, whose theatrical company has come to Moscow to perform *Hamlet,* watches him, too. And though he fails to fool her, he does charm her into send-ing him a new outfit that she has custom-tailored by a posh Lon-don clothier. The irony with which he charms her flows out of him. First of all, it has been starving for outlets amid the squalor and sleaze of cold-war Moscow. Next, as an idiom or rhetorical device that rests on limited expectations, it goes well with his threadbare existence. Without the distance afforded by irony, he would most likely see himself as a victim, an identity that could bring on self-pity and depression, perhaps even suicide.

According to Brantley, no one knows the uses of irony bet-ter than Bennett, who is so accomplished an ironist that even his irony-prone countrymen cannot keep pace with him: "Irony, a particularly gentle variety that by no means excludes compas-sion, is Mr. Bennett's element. . . . Even in his native England,

Mr. Bennett is perceived as unusually oblique."[25] Bennett's introduction to *Office Suite,* a double bill first televised in 1978,
claims that, like Guy Burgess of *An Englishman Abroad,* North-
of-Englanders use irony as a survival mechanism: "Hopes are
doomed to be dashed, expectations not to be realized, because
that's the way God, who certainly speaks with a southern ac-
cent, has arranged things."[26] But England's damp, cold attic offers rewards to the wary. The northerner who cultivates
self-deprecation will not fall as far as the optimist from Kent or
Sussex who is puffed up with high hopes. Feeling like an underdog or stepchild may even relieve stress. If northerners succeed
in life, they can argue that they overcame their baleful environment by dint of moral character. They can also claim that their
blue-collar origins, contrary to popular belief, provided the seed-
bed from which strong, healthy shoots like them can sprout. On
this score, Bennett has confessed that his pride in his background
amounts to "a mild form of inverted snobbery" (*WH* 386).

But if irony provides comforting alternatives as well as com-
pensations, it rarely conduces to joy. The question matters because joy surpasses by far adjusting to what is disagreeable or
settling for second best. Bennett grazed this issue while discussing the poet Louis MacNeice: "Irony stops you from being whole-
hearted, stops you from going overboard. But, of course, if you
don't go overboard, you tend not to make a splash" (*PM* 78).
Bennett has returned to the zone of Kafkan duality. Irony is a
way of hedging one's bets; it provides the comforts of safety
and control. Being of two minds about something or someone
can head off pain, but it also works as a preemptive strike. A
brake against abandon, it bridles decisiveness. The safety catch

of irony blocks the inertia created by conviction, faith, or the lyrical impulse to surrender. But the cool poise of the ironist is fragile. What irony induces if leaned on too heavily is an intense self-consciousness encroaching on anxiety, a fear that cannot be localized or named and thus eased. Because the skin disorder vexing Franz in *The Insurance Man* (1986) defies diagnosis, it costs him the compensation benefits given to those with work-related injuries. The bureaucracy casts deep shadows elsewhere in Bennett. Arthur Dodsworth of *A Visit from Miss Prothero* (1978) has been adapting well to two big losses—the death of his wife of many years and the retirement that took away the self-validation of work routine. What with his pottery classes, the class in cooking he looks forward to taking, and visits from the grandchildren, he has found contentment. But a visit from a nasty ex-colleague who tells him about changes in office policy and procedure that have been installed by the firm he served for thirty years unhinges him. Likewise, the retiring Headmaster in *Forty Years On* winces at his younger successor's proposed innovations.

The Headmaster's pain shows that people's defenses, even the ones they believe to be firmly in place, are thin. As in Kafka, the individual in Bennett often wavers between feeling puny and feeling singled out to suffer. The mean, grotty streets of Leeds adjoining the action of many of Bennett's plays teem with people fretting over being exposed, shamed, or caught off guard. Though these people are more odd than menacing, they inject undertones of dread into their surroundings. They become natural victims. Like Joseph K of Kafka's *The Trial* (1925), who engineers his own downfall, Bennett's people can defeat their best chances.

Their self-consciousness conjures up those Audenesque horrors
lurking around the corner ready to pounce. Lacking a sure sense
of self, they seek refuge in irony, but to no avail: irony for them
only promotes that awareness reflecting on awareness that freezes
action and smudges the rich, throbbing world with darkness and
doubt.

CHAPTER TWO

Ho, to Be in England

John Lahr has shown how Bennett's character-driven, socially relevant plays combine social change with personal crisis and also economic or professional opportunity with moral dislocation and stress: "Bennett strikes a deep chord in English life not so much by the stories he tells as the voice he tells them in. . . . He is a master of mood and social detail. . . . Shy and hermetic, Bennett is a man of abdications, whose comic tone sounds the true note of stalemate and resignation in English society."[1] If partisan politics impinge on Bennett's work, it is only to set a scene or jump-start a plot; the details are left hazy. What concerns him is the interplay of human dignity and the irony his people deploy to fend off loss and limitation. This counterpoint can evoke the hellish places of the mind and the depths of the soul's terrors. But the evocation usually occurs glancingly, often through chance references. Bennett writes well-observed, understated dramas of anguish leavened by humor. His province is the mist and smoke of the human psyche. In the collections of one-act plays, *Office Suite* and *Talking Heads,* relationships often thrive on indirection. The quiescent can also leap to life, proving that the people have been leading inner lives the whole time they have been on stage. Recently widowed Muriel Carpenter of *Soldiering On* (1987) has enough money to live very comfortably. But this talking head lets her crooked son cheat her out of her inheritance to assuage the unvoiced guilt she feels for having wrecked her daughter's life.

Family is a caution in Bennett. Taking up from Chekhov and Terence Rattigan, he writes about people unable to live either apart or together. Usually, they are family members who either bore or destroy each other out of love or loneliness in a country that has lost direction. The clash of desires or aims often moves to the fore of a Bennett script, like *A Private Function.* The people in this 1984 screenplay try to read and sometimes meet each other's needs. They rarely succeed. Though fulfilling, sex in the film also serves as a way of gaining power, like money. And most of Bennett's people *are* preoccupied with power, if only indirectly. Bennett conjures pathos and sometimes fun out of their inability either to better themselves or to move closer to one another. The prevalence of hospitals and cemeteries in Bennett's canon invokes this failure. In his introduction to *Objects of Affection,* Bennett notes, "In such unhelpful circumstances it's hardly surprising that several of the characters end up dead" (*OA* 7). The threat of death lingers. The main figures of *A Chip in the Sugar* and *A Private Function* have mothers in their seventies. The seventy-five-year-old Doris, from *A Cream Cracker under the Settee,* sits immobilized near her front inside door, where she will probably die, having sent away a policeman who offered her help. Women remain at risk. The main character's mother-in-law in *Getting On* is dying, and a dead woman is carried from the stage in *The Old Crowd.* Connie Craven of *Enjoy* has lost her memory, and her husband, Wilfred, the victim of a hit-and-run driver, is paralyzed below the neck. Incapacitated, infirm fathers do die in both *Intensive Care* and *Rolling Home.* Like those in *Soldiering On, Marks, Rolling*

Home, and perhaps both *A Visit from Miss Prothero* and *A Woman of No Importance* (1982), Wilfred probably molested a family intimate.

He is only one of many failures in Bennett. Mollie Panter-Downes, in her "Letter from London" column for the *New Yorker,* calls Hilary of *The Old Country* (1977) a "failed traitor."[2] She is right. Speaking from his dacha outside of Moscow, this ex-Foreign Office chief who gave top-grade secrets to the Soviets welcomes any chance to discuss, with deep affection, the England he betrayed. So nostalgic is he that, when told to return home as part of a spy swap, he agrees, even though he knows that he will have to stand trial as a traitor. Guy Burgess of *An Englishman Abroad* fails just as badly. Like Hilary before him, the best explanation he can give for his treachery is that it seemed to be the right policy to adopt at the time. He betrayed his country mainly because he liked the secrecy betrayal bestowed. Every day at work he would gloat over the ignorance of colleagues who had no idea of his actions. "Burgess was a spy because he wanted a place where he was alone, and . . . having a secret supplies this" (*WH* 211), said Bennett in the play's introduction. But as the action unfolds, Burgess lets on that his unmasking by Whitehall took place so long ago that it is now a dead issue.

George III of *Madness* has failed, too. The 1788 outbreak of insanity portrayed by Nigel Hawthorne on both stage and screen was but one of several suffered by the king. In fact, George spent his last decade or so isolated and insane, far from the seat of government. Thus his recovery at the end of the Bennett scripts was merely temporary; his porphyria—if indeed he was suffer-

ing from porphyria—had merely run its course. As revolutionary and apparently successful as it was, Dr. Willis's cure may
have had nothing to do with George's return to sanity.

The royal crisis in *Madness* calls to mind the domestic strife
actuating the works Bennett set in contemporary England. He
slights the drug-ridden slums and gun-happy streets of today's
megalopolis along with the greed, rampant consumerism, and
pollution created by industry. What rivets him instead is the concept of the family as a fusion of devotion and misunderstanding,
of breakdown and persistence. The tensions of family living
prime impulses of aggressiveness. Though natural, flare-ups that
follow moments of stress breach his characters' sense of themselves as decent, moral people. The womanizing Arthur
Wicksteed of *Habeas Corpus* (1973) insults his son, Dennis,
along with his wife by proposing a tryst with the young woman
Dennis is dating. The sudden urge to maim and bruise overtakes
lonely, repressed Marjory of the telescript *Marks* when her son,
Leslie, comes home with a tattoo, an indelible sign of vulgarity
that drives home to her the hopelessness of rising from the working class. Leslie reminds her of his tattooed father, a ne'er-do-
well who bolted the family years earlier. The reminder infuriates
Marjory. She shrieks at her son. But the incident plays on—longer
than either of them could have imagined. Leslie answers
Marjory's outburst by hitting her in the face, showing him his
dangerous side. He is both frightened and disgusted. To banish
those forbidden impulses awakened by love, he denies his heart.
He has been repelled by the idea of hating someone he loves.
Better to sink his feelings, he believes, than to vent the wrath
that can do irreparable harm.

HO, TO BE IN ENGLAND

His mother may soon put him out of the house. Sons whose very existence is denied by their parents come to light in *Enjoy* and *Say Something Happened* (1982). But whereas the Rhodeses of *Something* ignore their retarded son, they wince at the discovery that their daughter, Margaret, would not break her fun to come home and care for them if they became disabled. (The motif recurs in *Intensive Care.*) Perhaps Margaret is also cringing from the savagery that family dynamics could set going.

I

Bennett sets most of his work in the North of England, where he was born and grew up. He knows the place, feels comfortable there, and expands into its folkways and linguistic patterns. "The language and the rhythms of northern speech came naturally to me" (*OA* 7), he said in 1982. Yet the woes caused by northern families in plays like *Enjoy* and *Marks* show that any nostalgia he feels for Leeds has not clouded his insight into his ex-neighbors' capacity for evil. The same truth holds good for people everywhere. Regardless of where they are from, his people disclose the same salt edge. Though based in Kafka's Prague, *The Insurance Man* enacts the same ugly office politics shown in both the London-set *One Fine Day* (1979) and *Office Suite,* a double bill that unfolds in the North. Bennett is fascinated by the factions and rivalries that crop up among coworkers and sometimes among those of different ranks in the bureaucracy, along with their occasional stabs at fraternization. Nowhere does he demonize, trivialize, or promote any ideas or social programs. Frank Rich uses King George and Peggy Schofield (of the *Talk-*

ing Heads monologue *A Woman of No Importance*) to argue that Bennett's comedies "may be crowd-pleasers but [they are also] subversive, . . . depicting lost souls who seem to emblemize an unhappy England that cannot diagnose, let alone cure, its ills."[3]

Some of this important work comes from Bennett. No polemicist, he lacks a guiding theory and perhaps even a ground plan of ideas. But if he offers no practical agenda, he does provide both an orientation and a rallying point. As is seen in *A Bed among the Lentils* (1987), the industrial West's capitalism knits well with religion and family life. Yet the three systems can also clash, mostly because capitalism tends to replace cooperation and compassion with the creed of self. Since this maneuver can also lead to anarchy, capitalism requires strict laws enforced by strong judicial and police systems. There are no judges in Bennett. And *A Private Function* is his only work featuring policemen, one of whom is on the take. In place of programs, Bennett substitutes a conservative belief in stability, order, and guidelines within which goals should be pursued; crime, he believes, stems more from personal choice than from social forces. His wrongdoers are not passive victims who have inherited bad genes or a bad environment. They feel wronged themselves. His happiest people, conversely, have learned tolerance of themselves and others. Avoiding excessive hopes, the title figure of *Our Winnie* (1982) and the chiropodist Gilbert Chilvers of *A Private Function* trim down their expectations to bring them in line with reality. As Arthur Dodsworth learns in *A Visit from Miss Prothero,* contentment is fragile and fleeting. But it *can* be savored. Those who make excessive demands never know it. Like Peggy

Prothero, they do see it in others, though, and they both resent and try to smash it.

This kind of conflict intrigues Bennett. Whether writing about firms, families, or spies, he prefers the personal, the local, and the intimate over the theoretical and the doctrinaire. While frustration and loss drive some of his people either to pervert love and order or to seek these goals in remote ideals, the truest visions in his work take root in small delights, plainspoken decency, and respect for others. This steadfastness helps Bennett find poignancy, pathos, and a redeeming grace in the everyday. "When people are on their best behaviour they aren't always at their best," he says in *Writing Home* (32), repeating the point later in the book (336) and again in *A Question of Attribution.*[4] Catching people off guard brings better insights than posing them and letting them mouth rehearsed moralities. The techniques that promote the spontaneous over the prearranged create flexibility elsewhere, too. Anecdotes are sometimes left unfinished once their larger point is made. And some of these larger points fall short of fulfilling the promise made for them. But Bennett has not misled anyone. What can count most in a Bennett play is not the central plot but the throwaway images that sneak in at the sides. These details, though often forgotten after getting a laugh, carry a fair measure of a play's moral weight, helping depict the emotional ransacking of a King George or an elderly Leeds householder.

Though Bennett writes about uneasiness and guilt with sharp unsentimentality, he is no scold. He relishes his people, an oddball group of eccentrics, some of them ugly, some attractive, all human. Any creative writer's main task consists of lending the commonplace importance. Bennett's ability to suggest a wealth of motivation along with a fullness of inner life, even in his minor figures, recalls Raymond Carver's sensitivity to the awareness flooding the everyday. Bennett's calling himself a snob (*WH* 86, 120, 133), though typically self-deprecating, is unjust. His long essay, "The Lady in the Van" (*WH* 59–94), about Miss Shepherd, who lived for fifteen years in a series of vans parked in his Camden Town garden, brims with affection. Though he loses patience with this "pathetic scarecrow" (*WH* 62), he is always surprised when he starts patronizing her, stumbling on a revelation that makes patronizing impossible. His avoidance of superior airs helps him unearth other finds that touch his heart, like her girlhood piano studies in Paris and the brief novitiate she later served in a London convent.

He did let Miss Shepherd live on his property rent-free for fifteen years, during which time he did much of her shopping and ran an electrical current from his house into her van to give her light and heat. But perhaps he owes her more than she does him. She helped him find poetry in the shabby and the rundown. She also showed him that he can write as keenly about old age as he can about youth and that he is as comfortable moving among the poor as among the rich and powerful. Patrick Skene Catling has tallied the rewards of his gift for immersing himself in the prosaic: "He is the dramatist of the humdrum without humbug. The plebeian ordinariness of many of his characters and the banality of their speech invest his plays with the extraordinary excitement of universal revelation. Prosaic experiences are made to seem significantly poetic."[5] The poetry comes from Bennett's wit, alertness, and empathy. As he showed in "The Lady in the Van," he is open to surprise, and he has a well-honed sense of the journalistic moment. His close attention to details in matters of character and feeling discloses in him a heart knowledge rare in a satirist. One of the best acting roles in Bennett's works, the eponym of *Our Winnie* gains the audience's love along with its respect despite being a retarded mute.

Winnie has the moral clarity and consistency Bennett admires; content to govern her life by a handful of truths and ties, she need not call attention to herself or back down from anyone. Her wordless self-presence calls to mind a sentence from Kafka's *Trial* quoted by Bennett in his essay "Kafka in Las Vegas": "The verdict doesn't come all at once; the proceedings gradually merge into the verdict" (*WH* 346). Quietly canny with an intelligence that glows rather than glitters, Bennett writes about epiphanies that make life comprehensible and bearable. He indicted himself unfairly by saying in the introduction to his 1991 stage version of *The Wind in the Willows,* "My theatrical imagination is pretty limited."[6] Following the example of Chekhov, he delays making his points in favor of rendering the texture of life.

Yes, the spectacular makes a mighty splash when it occurs. But eventually life returns to its everydayness. And this daily existence interests Bennett most of all. Receiving a bespoke suit cheers Guy Burgess in *An Englishman Abroad.* But he is wearing it in grungy Moscow, not in the London he pines for. He knows enough, though, to stop pining, as is seen in his gait. He is not merely slogging through Moscow's snow. His jaunty step, his look of self-assurance, and the strains of Gilbert and Sullivan's "For He Is an Englishman" brightening the soundtrack as the camera picks him up all fuse into one of those spots of time in which nothing happens but everything is revealed. Bennett's mastery of the small but telling comic gesture lights the way through a tangle of complex emotional states and glimpses the larger truth.

To give a fresh comic slant, he'll align incongruities in parallel syntax. The sentence logic uncoiling from these combinations, if delivered with the right vocal emphasis, can seize a theater audience. One can imagine the attention focused on John Gielgud's Headmaster in *Forty Years On* as he recited the following lines in his farewell speech to his students: "Thirty years ago today, Tupper, the Germans marched into Poland and you're picking your nose. See me afterwards" (*Plays One* 29). These lines convey the tension animating the play; the heroic and the mean, the historical and the personal, always compete for attention. Both Bennett's eye for detail and his flair for clarity, color, and bounce have served him well. The crispness and gloss conveyed by the play within a play that develops the plot clash with the grimness of Bennett's vision. This counterpoint, one of Bennett's favorite devices, works well in *Forty Years On*. Besides holding the audience, it smooths the play's texture, stops the plot from peaking too early, and creates opportunities for fun. The fun can take different forms. In the midst of the same long speech in which Tupper is rebuked, the gravity generated by the Headmaster's sonorities is punctuated when a teacher blows his nose loudly.

Bennett knows the importance of controlling audience response. A character addresses the audience in the second scene of *Kafka's Dick* to explain that we are watching a play, not reality. Max Brod's aside breaks dramatic drive in favor of creating critical distance at a time when the audience might otherwise be swept emotionally into the action. The same kind of Brechtian alienation occurs in the stage directions preceding the first scene of *Enjoy*. A familiar phrase from Handel's *Messiah* stops after attaining "full flow" (*Plays One* 265). Then, during his description of the Cravens' sitting room, Bennett notes, "There should be something not quite right" (*Plays One* 265) about the set. Foreshadowing in *Enjoy* also divides the human issue from the action. When Wilfred Craven pauses in his long plea to accompany his daughter, Linda, to Kuwait, her response, "I wasn't listening" (*Plays One* 290), shows him that he never figured in her plans for the future and that he should have known it. Linda never makes it to Kuwait. But the possibility that she will reveal her reasons for excluding her father sharpens the audience's attention as the play's second act nears.

Another attention-getter that Bennett uses effectively is the device of delayed exposition. Midway into the 1978 one-acter *A Visit from Miss Prothero,* the following exchange takes place:

MR. DODSWORTH: I'm sorry. Your mother died.
MISS PROTHERO: She didn't die. Father killed her.[7]

If spoken with the right measure of matter-of-factness, Peggy Prothero's line will stir an audience into rethinking its earlier impressions both of her behavior and of the motivations behind it. But if Bennett knows the benefits of retarding or derailing a play's forward drive by interweaving elements of exposition and complication, he's also a dab hand at rising to crescendos. Part 1 of the two-part *The Madness of George III* (1991) ends with a strong visual image buttressed by music. As the struggling king is forced into his restraining chair, his arms and hands immobilized, he howls wildly. Then his captors stand free of him. The timing of George's appalling enthronement has coincided with the climax of Handel's *Coronation Anthem.*

Bennett uses his fine command of the physical aspects of theater to gain laughter as well as pathos. At the end of act 1 of *Kafka's Dick,* the actors collide while trying to stop a resurrected Kafka from seeing his name on the spines of the books in an admirer's library. It is easy to disparage this flurry of action as slapstick or knockabout. But this disparagement is wrongheaded; both the inventiveness of the script that occasioned it and the immaculate timing of the actors that make it work deserve praise, not rebuke. Another example of Bennett's sure sense of stagecraft comes in the music that peppers his scripts. Songs like *South Pacific's* "I'm in Love with a Wonderful Guy," the playing of which ends *Me, I'm Afraid of Virginia Woolf,* and "Goodnight, Ladies," which accompanies the departure from the stage of a female corpse in *The Old Crowd,* have been well known for years to most theatergoers. Their familiarity provides a brilliant auditory shorthand, capturing the songs' ironic relevance to the onstage action.

This recognition gives pleasure. It also blends with the obliqueness of Bennett's dramatic technique. Bennett enjoys approaching his subjects at an angle rather than head on, developing the importance of something he sees out of the corner of his eye. This indirection gives his work an impromptu look that sends the mind to Harold Pinter. Apparently aimless talk in a play like the Kafka-driven *Insurance Man* can take on an anguished intensity. Loneliness pervades both tone and subject in Bennett, even though much of his work unfolds within immediate families. The speed with which characters' reserves often shatter gives the plays the ambience of a nightmare. Despite their many images of domesticity, Bennett's plays are haunted by isolation. Connie Craven of *Enjoy* keeps asking her husband where their daughter has gone. Either her memory is bad or she's trying to deny the truth that Linda has left the country. Ironically, there is no truth for her to deny. Despite Dad's insistence that Linda has gone to Sweden, she remains right in town.

Married couples in Bennett can devise concealment operations that rival those in Pinter, so fragile and desperate are the links joining them. The talking head Susan of *Bed among the Lentils* never discusses her "rare and desiccated [erotic] conjunctions" (*TH* 30) with her vicar-husband, Geoffrey. Neither does that other supposed mainstay of their shared life, religion, ever come under discussion. In fact, she does not even know if Geoffrey believes in God. And she won't ask, lest she disturb the delicate balance that keeps them together. Bennett deserves his reputation of writing quiet, gracefully shadowed plays. Despite his flair for the histrionic gesture, he usually walks his people through a gray haze. Undergirding these muted tonalities is often a substratum of tension and resentment that could cave in at any time. Bennett's unabashedly funny, morally searching plays challenge the imagination; the action unfolding on the stage may only graze the one developing in the subtext. Any playwright who sets such a risky course for himself commands respect. And Bennett has it. When one of his plays nears its climax, his technique will be equal to the event.

II

Forty Years On, the first play in the 1997 collection *Plays One,* crackles with Wildean wit. One can easily imagine Lady Bracknell of *The Importance of Being Earnest* (1895) responding to a good-morning greeting with the one-liner "The weather is immaterial" (*Plays One* 40). Another early play, *Habeas Corpus,* wrests humor from a non sequitur couched as a syllogism. A housemaid is speaking, most likely in a flat, toneless voice: "Doctors can touch anybody, because they don't have feelings to go with it. That's what they go to medical school for" (*Plays One* 104). The play remains alert to the benefits of incongruity. The following ditty, for instance, to be sung to the tune of "The Isle of Capri," juxtaposes the familiar and the casual with raciness and desperation:

'Twas on the A43 that I met him.
We just had a day by the sea.
Now he's gone, and he's left me expecting.
Will somebody, please, marry me. (202)

When Bennett sees the chance to extend or enrich a scene, his rhythmical, figured style delivers for him. Even his nondramatic prose can unleash a memorable emotion-charged image, like the following description of a military graveyard in Flanders: "The low walls are sharp and new-looking, unblurred by creeper. There is no lichen on the gravestones, the dead seeming not to have fertilized the ground so much as sterilized it" (*WH* 28). The eye for significant everyday detail disclosed by the description validates William Carlos Williams's claim, from *In the American Grain* (1925), that an attentive look at the specific will evoke the universal: death's only offspring is death.

What is more, the evocation will look unforced. Bennett gains both the attention and the support of theatergoers by being so graceful and approachable. Even his aphorisms unleash wit while avoiding malice. Wit could easily fuel the imagination of a playwright who enjoys making people laugh as much as Bennett does: "I first realized I could make people laugh and liked doing it" (*WH* 18), he said of his undergraduate self. But his ability to modulate his wit enhances its effectiveness. Works like *An Englishman Abroad* and *Madness* describe anguish without forfeiting humor or stumbling into the traps of mawkishness or irreverence. The clarity of Bennett's prose hides an extraordinary craftsmanship, the easy flow of the dialogue belying the good ear, the hard work, and the training infusing it. Alert but unpretentious, his shrewd prose tallies with his belief in sanity, reserve, and fairness to others. Those with a sense of fun, even the subversive kind, who frown on recklessness and extravagance in favor of reasonable expectations reasonably met will relish his company.

CHAPTER THREE

Some Uses of History

Studying history at Oxford for seven years helped build and refine Bennett's skill as a dramatist. Even though the research that underlay *The Madness of George III* (1991) was Bennett's first sustained effort of its kind in twenty years, history infuses at least one of his works from each of the past four decades, including the skits from BTF. The historical perspective shifted, as could be expected in a playwright who turned his hand to films and television scripts over his writing career. What holds steady is Bennett's imaginative intent. Like Brecht, he uses historical drama to ask where we are, how we got here, and what we should do next. Underlying these big questions is an awareness of the possibility that people in the last quarter of the twentieth century lack positive goals, a possibility that invites the further conjecture that the present is inferior to the past.

Such conjectures neither thicken nor clog Bennett's scripts. Though he may draw artistic inspiration from the court of George III or from Leeds's slums in 1980, his plays taken together as a group seem really to deal with the joys of playwriting itself. He enjoys setting himself challenges. The two *Madness* works, for instance, exclude certain historical figures, give others more prominence than they had in real life, and distort the motives of still others. By changing history, Bennett can clarify the social and moral offshoots of George's madness. The changes follow no pattern. Thus the real-life Queen Charlotte was "every bit as homely and parsimonious" as she appears on stage.[1] Bennett

made the statesman Dundas younger in the play than in real life
because William Pitt, George's prime minister, would be more
likely to confide in someone his age than in an elder (*MGIII*
xvii). Bennett also points out that the Prince of Wales, heir apparent to the crown, was "a more genial character than presented
here and more reluctant to have it admitted in public or in the
press that his father might be mad" (*MGIII* xi). Since stage drama
thrives on opposition, Bennett's besmirching of the prince helped
sharpen battle lines with the ailing king. Yet Bennett is too honest to push historical evidence further than it should go. Both his
timing and his judgment in his handling of the historical record
can be flawless. No slave to fact, he knows the point at which to
reveal that the apparently false is true.

I

Bennett's instinct for the right moment goes with a daz-
zling economy of means. Reviewing *Forty Years On* (1968) in
the *New York Times,* Irving Wardle called it "a full-scale mock-
heroic pageant of modern British myth" that uses the secondary
school where the pageant unfolds as "an image of Britain at the
crossroads."[2] Wardle's description hints at the ambitiousness of
Bennett's first full-length stage play. *Forty* is not merely the work
of a brilliant young playwright with a gift for sparkling dialogue
and scene shifting; it also reveals the working-class northerner
looking to entrench himself, without straining, as a wry, sophisticated observer of upper-class southern foibles. Only after win-
ning his spurs as a nonchalant critic of the follies of London and
Oxbridge chic could he return to his Yorkshire roots. In his In-

troduction to *Writing Home,* Bennett tells how the brittle, high-luster social comedy of *Forty* freed him to explore his psyche as a provincial. Just before saying that "Art comes out of art," he notes that the work "has much more to do with art than with life" (*WH* xii).

Like a Chekhov play, *Forty* features a leave-taking or goodbye. It opens on the last day of the school year at Albion House, a faded public school in the South of England that stands as "a loose metaphor for England" (*Plays One* 7) itself. The day also marks the end of active service for the school's Headmaster, who is about to say farewell to the faculty, staff, and student body of Albion, with which he has been connected, as both boy and master, for fifty years. Following the speech will be the traditional end-of-term play, which is sited in Albion's "dingy and dark and somewhat oppressive" (*Plays One* 27) Assembly Hall. The rest of the scenes unfold in the basement of the swank London hotel Claridge's between 1939 and 1945, when the building was serving as an air-raid shelter. Also on stage is a lectern from which several set pieces, or memoirs, are spoken, often with the enhancement (or comic distraction) provided by the slides shown on a back-projection screen. These set pieces include passages taken verbatim from English highbrow writers like Leonard Woolf, Osbert Sitwell, and Harold Nicholson. Lighthearted mandarin nonsense abounds, as is seen in a supposed recollection of the splendors of Virginia Woolf's Sunday morning "soirées" (*Plays One* 74), spoken by the Junior Master Charles Tempest, a role played in the original production by Bennett himself: "There by the window talking to Leonard and Virginia were the Berlins, Irving and Isaiah. And then there was Virginia herself elegant and quizzical, those great nostrils quivering in the sunlight playing over her long pale face. She never used cosmetics, except to powder her nose. But then she had her father's nose" (74).

The script's play within a play, or second play, which covers key moments in recent English history, shows different generations questioning the values of their predecessors as a prelude to self-assessment. Bennett has commented on the structural unity he wanted the second play, *Speak for England, Arthur,* to lend to the action: "The form of *Forty Years On* is more complicated than I would dream of attempting now. It is a play within a play in which the time scale of the first play gradually catches up with the time scale of the second, one cog the years 1900–39, the other 1939–45, and both within the third wheel of the present day" (*Plays One* 9–10). The first play occupies the object level; it is self-contained, autonomous, and independent of the audience. *Arthur* stands as a gloss on this main action. It does not stand alone. An earlier modern play built along the lines of *Forty,* Thornton Wilder's *Skin of Our Teeth* (1942), also used the device of the interior play. What goes on at the metalevel in this American play finds echoes with and even intersects with the main action besides commenting on it. But the points of intersection appear more often, and the echoes sounding from the interplay of object level and metalevel boom more loudly in *Forty,* as they do in Pirandello's *Henry IV* (1922). Because the roles in *Arthur* are played by members of the Albion House community, identities may slide into each other or clash. Often, the roles played by the Albion people comment sharply on real-life situations.

The area where life's nastiness intrudes most often is that of the public school, with its stated code of honor, decency, and fair play. Bennett's satire on British boarding-school education would have touched a nerve in any public school old boy (or alumnus) watching the play. In most cases, the old boy would have either laughed or winced with embarrassment or pain. Scenes like the one in which the school's nanny says goodnight to one of the boys recall the dark turns taken by *If* . . . (1969), a film directed by Lindsay Anderson, who would later direct Bennett' s telescript *The Old Crowd* (1979): "Give us a kiss. Kisses make babies grow. Night, night, sleep tight. God bless and go to sleep or the policeman'll come and cut your little tail off" (*Plays One* 48). Shocks like this come often in *Forty,* Bennett showing that the English public school, seduced by its wishful self-image, has for decades, if not centuries, been making claims for itself that cannot be supported. Some of the play's subversiveness, along with Bennett's behind-the-scenes persona of cool knowing insider, comes through in Stephen Schiff's critique: "Scatology, private parts, the whole panoply of stuff that makes sixth graders giggle—this has always been a kind of obsession in Bennett's work. For good reason: it is the embarrassing secret we all have in common. . . . [Bennett] is, in short, the poet of embarrassment."[3] Scatology governs Bennett's portrayal of British public school education as fragmented, disturbed, and dirty. Mud pelts all the system's insiders. "I wish I could put my hands on the choir's parts" (*Plays One* 34), says Tempest while looking for the musical score of *Arthur.* More pointedly, there is the scene midway through the play's second act in which Mr. Franklin, a housemaster and the retiring Headmaster's successor, plays a teacher who tries to seduce a boy. So pointed is the scene's dialogue, in fact, that an indignant Headmaster halts the proceedings. Another reminder of the homosexuality infiltrating Albion House occurs with two boys named Skinner and Tupper. Tupper's name strikes a chord with the ugliness of Iago's description in *Othello* (act 1, scene 1, lines 88–89) of Desdemona's wedding night-activities to her father: "An old black ram / Is tupping your white ewe."

While also invoking the flesh, Skinner's name foreshadows that of a bisexual male in Bennett's 1978 television play *Me, I'm Afraid of Virginia Woolf*. The foreshadowing is apt. The Headmaster (who was played by John Gielgud) interrupts his farewell speech at the outset to stop Skinner from "playing with the hair of the boy in front" of him (*Plays One* 29). Have not writers like Donne, Ibsen, and Dylan Thomas used hair as a sexual symbol? And who is the boy whose hair has intrigued Skinner? A couple of minutes later, Tempest stops Skinner and Tupper from sitting together (*Plays One* 32). Perhaps their unions are as familiar to the faculty as to the boys. In one of those asides that take precedence over the line of thought they interrupt, the Headmaster pauses in his prayer to the boys to advise Tupper, "you won't find him down there" (*Plays One* 52). If Tupper was looking for Skinner, his search ends quickly. One boy is either sitting on the shoulders or straddling the back of the other while impersonating in drag Lady Ottoline Morrell during a chat with Bertrand Russell. Tupper was probably looking for Skinner during the Headmaster's sermon. When the Headmaster says that he suspected Tupper's being "at the bottom of" the Ottoline Morrell impersonation, Skinner tells him, "No. He was the top, sir. I was the bottom" (*Plays One* 59).

In its theatricality, *Forty* recalls the skits, monologues, and songs that made BTF so much fun earlier in the 1960s. At times, the play's fledgling author seems to be flexing his artistic muscles by shaping different kinds of material to suit his purposes—that is, provoking laugher while pondering the meaning of England's past. The structural looseness of the work, one that is "as much a revue as a play," has made it, among other things, "an elaborate life support system for the preservation of bad jokes" (*Plays One* 10). These jokes take so many forms and tumble so quickly on each other's heels that nearly every line of dialogue can make audiences laugh. Bennett's model for this cascading wit is Wilde's *The Importance of Being Earnest,* a fact he never tries to hide. Thus it's no surprise to hear a character say, "All women dress like their mothers, that is their tragedy. No man ever does. That is his" (*Plays One* 41). A minute before Lady Dundown said these lines, which come nearly verbatim from Wilde's 1895 play, she rose from her wheelchair with the words, "I can walk. It's just that I'm so rich I don't need to" (*Plays One* 41). The play's comedy is richly varied. Besides using sight gags or visual jokes, Bennett will have characters repeat each other's words, or he injects a note of nonsense, often phrased parallel to a previous statement. Tempest's observation, "Here, here is Sargent's portrait of the Lavery Sisters," elicits the response, all the funnier for coming from an aging Tory blue blood, "And here, oh here, is Landseer's portrait of the Andrews Sisters" (*Plays One* 46); the truth that the Andrews Sisters were no beauties takes comic force from the truth that E. H. Landseer survives largely as a painter of dogs.

So smoothly do these little routines knit with the action of *Forty* that they nearly make the play a primer on stage comedy. Their sparkle also makes it tempting to cite more examples.

SOME USES OF HISTORY

Bennett has enough faith in his sense of humor to break the momentum of *Forty* to intrude either a joke or a funny set piece. In act 1, he presents a disquisition on the fatness of Edward VII as a history lesson. Some minutes later, as soon as a picture of Lawrence of Arabia appears on the screen, the Headmaster starts lecturing: "T. E. Lawrence, the man and the myth. Which is the man and which is myth . . . ? What is truth and what is fable? Where is Ruth and where is Mabel?" (*Plays One* 55). Such winsome absurdities hide the direction the play or even a vignette will take. A minute or so after the Headmaster's rhymed couplet, a picture of the desert replaces the one of Lawrence—except (in what is perhaps a borrowing from Kingsley Amis's *Lucky Jim* [1954] and/or Iris Murdoch's *Sandcastle* [1957]), the new image is upside down. "Some of us are a little too old to stand on our heads, Crabtree. Thank you," says the Headmaster to the operator of the slide carousel before resuming the lecture (Plays *One* 55). Besides helping the Headmaster segue neatly to his lecture notes, the icy dryness of his remark elicits a chuckle from the audience that complements, rather than competes with, the laughs roused by the inverted picture of the desert.

The comic mood keeps shifting. The volley of witty improprieties on unrelated topics that occurs near the start of act 2 owes much to the style developed by *That Was the Week That Was* (TW3) earlier in the 1960s. TW3 probably owed a still greater debt to BTF, which Bennett helped found and build. Then there are the ribald songs, the comic edge of which sharpens by being sung to tunes like "Hark the Herald Angels Sing" and "The Church's One Foundation." The singers of this second tune, a choir of rugby players who appear unexpectedly on stage, threaten to disjoint matters. But Bennett springs another surprise. Rather than fragmenting the action, the rugger hearties augment it, for about five minutes, anyway. During their second song, they not only pass a rugby ball among themselves but also pretend to throw the ball into the audience.

Forty has as many stoppages and digressions as a Robert Altman film. Though densely theatrical, the play is not dramatic, with Bennett breaking dramatic momentum at will. Following the example of Pirandello's *Each in His Own Way* (1924), the second act takes place during the intermission, or interval, between scenes of the play within a play. The players from the earlier scenes, having reverted to their original roles, lounge around and talk casually. Back on stage, a character may forget a line. More than once, the Headmaster drops out of his role to object to the impropriety of a scene. If Bennett disapproves of the Headmaster's stuffiness, he nonetheless gives it the chance to declare itself. Blocking dramatic drive postpones the climax he seems to be building to. This strategy also conveys his satire as a series of images and counterimages. Any poignancy that emerges dissolves quickly, sometimes in a non sequitur. Or a character who is voicing his deepest emotions discovers that nobody is listening to him. A prisoner of war sends his parents a letter made up mostly of trivia and jokes.

The letter helps set the play's tone. War remains a presence, but a comic one, with Bennett sacrificing emotion to jest. For example, the presence on stage of gas masks, which were standard issue to Londoners during World War II, the roar of the *Luftwaffe* overhead, and the voice of Neville Chamberlain all remind the audience of the courage displayed during the Blitz

SOME USES OF HISTORY

by their parents' generation. Yet Chamberlain's trial is played for laughs. Appearing in the dock holding the umbrella he carried getting off the plane after his notorious 1938 appeasement flight to Munich, he faces charges, not of treason, but of indecent exposure—at a window of his Downing Street residence, no less. The mood of the trial is either enhanced or shattered by a fox-trot the defense counsel dances with the bursar's secretary during the interrogation.

The dance is typical. Something is happening on stage all the time in *Forty*. The play's awareness of the nonverbal resources of the theater makes for a very rich evening, and this richness is neither casual nor random. Unity in *Forty* stems from the forward march of time, which asserts itself as the time frames of the first and second plays converge; from the similarities between England and Albion House School; and from the audience's knowledge of twentieth-century British history, particularly the contributions made to the development of the national psyche by figures like Winston Churchill and T. E. Lawrence. The audience also recognizes in the flow of events the imperative of change. Bennett wants the recognition to happen early. Two jet planes zoom overhead during the Headmaster's long farewell address that opens the play. Yet later in the first act, change is discredited. Coinciding with the appearance of the date 1900 on the hymn board in the school's Assembly Room is a speech that refutes the belief that life is lived by the clock or the calendar: "To enter upon the new century was not like opening a door and crossing a threshold. The old Queen was still alive, and when she died most of what she stood for lived on" (*Plays One* 39).

But change is inevitable, even if it bypasses the categories usually assigned to it. Is it to be welcomed? Any answer to this question should reckon with the great turn-of-the-century country houses with names like Grabbett, Lumber, and Clout that find their way into the script. These names are reminders that the elegance of Georgian England required abundant domestic labor, a reality that translated into long hours, low pay, and wretched working conditions for the servants of the rich. The play's incarnation of the old order is the Headmaster. But his only consistent feature is the ambiguity with which he is presented. Though "absent-minded, impulsive, out of touch" (*WH* 298), he has both the decency and the decisiveness to stop the action of *Arthur* when the play careens toward the troughs of pornography. In this regard, he stands as the play's only guardian of the civilized virtues. He is also saddened by the knowledge that many of these virtues, dear as they are to him, are rearguard and that his retirement is appropriate, if not overdue. "I am not sure of anything nowadays. I am lost. I am adrift" (*Plays One* 70), he says near the outset of act 2. But this elder who reels around the stage trying to get out of the other characters' way generates little pathos. When questioned about his future, he says that he intends to live near Albion House because he wants "to be within striking distance of the boys" (*Plays One* 66), and he also laments the passing, with his retirement, of archaic, sometimes sadistic Albion standbys like compulsory games and corporal punishment.

Forty fuses what Bennett both prizes and loathes. It tries to resolve the problem of why a practice or institution he knows to be ridiculous and hypocritical can nevertheless warm his heart.

He approaches the problem by claiming that parody and nostalgia in the play are very close (*WH* 259). Speaking at New York's Museum of Broadcasting's BBC Seminar series, he took a different tack. The complex emotional response of loving and hating, he said in November 1986, calls for irony, a trope with which he is well acquainted. In 1970, Bernard Levin discussed both the magnitude of the play's artistic challenge for Bennett and the failure of the play's audiences to accept the challenge. Though "widely misunderstood and dismissed," Levin said, the play performed "with astonishingly sure-footed skill the exceptionally difficult task . . . of facing both the future and the past calmly, with understanding and without self-deception."[4]

What Bennett learned by pitting the past against the present is unclear. No sooner does he make a serious value statement than, rather than developing it, he either makes fun of it or drops it. Sometimes, he registers approval in places where one might expect scorn. For instance, he says that the novelistic school of the clubman adventurer associated with right-wingers like Sapper and John Buchan "runs like a thread of good-class tweed through twentieth-century literature" (*Plays One* 81). Counterrhythm is another staple of *Forty*. During a radio broadcast of Churchill's speech to the British nation announcing the end of World War II, some students begin to fight. This incongruity puts forth the bitter truth that peace and humankind are incompatible; people always flail away at each other, even in the shadow of the olive branch.

Conversely, if incongruity will not go away, perhaps it can best be lived with as an object of ridicule. Such was the attitude of black humorists like John Guare in the late 1960s. Another literary school that sheds light on the play is absurdism. Though full of jokes, songs, and moments of wistful reminiscence, the play avoids congestion. Its lack of box-office appeal (*Plays One* 10) cannot be blamed on a throw-it-all-in style. In fact, the play is very selective, omitting all mention of the Beatles, the Black Power movement, Vietnam, or the God Is Dead theology, so popular at the time of the play's first staging, that made nearly everything permissible.

Nor, like Peter Weiss's *Marat/Sade* (1964), does *Forty* seek value in the moaning and writhing of the insane. It does follow Ionesco's *Bald Soprano* (1949), which is subtitled *An Anti-Play,* in putting drama to nondramatic uses. Qualifying as an antiplay in its own right, *Forty* also approaches meaning through the medium of irony, a rhetorical mode that has not broken down or gone stale from misuse. The play resolves nothing. But it does suggest ways in which resolution might occur. These suggestions suffice Bennett. With an epistemology whose modesty tugs against its belting theatricality, it provides splendid entertainment. Clive Barnes was far off target when he called the play a "cheap and nasty" effort further marred by "pretentiousness and ineptness."[5] Bennett's ability to hold audience attention, aided by his having created, in the Headmaster's role, a gift to any actor, tells why *Forty Years On* will be admired by friends of the theater despite the technical challenges imposed by its staging.

II

A Day Out, Bennett's first television play, ran into production problems different from those that have haunted *Forty Years On*. Filmed in black and white and first shown in December

SOME USES OF HISTORY

1972, the play was designed as "a gentle Edwardian idyll with intimations of the war to come" (*OA* 136). But the weather around Halifax, in southwest central Yorkshire, where the action unfolds, refused to cooperate. Certain scenes meant to take place in bright sunshine had to be rewritten to suit the unseasonable May doldrums. What the sun's refusal to shine could not mask, though, was Bennett's personal stamp. Like *Forty Years On, A Day Out* blends the dreamlike and the crunchy to gain access to the past. Even though the backward look it provides is more affectionate than that of its 1968 predecessor, it's scope also includes a large cast of characters whose interactions imply a sharp authorial awareness of the dangers of power. Also reflecting *Forty* is the teleplay's preoccupation with religion. All the action occurs on a Sunday, partly in a ruined abbey, where the members of a cycling club take lunch. Though they miss the weekly Sunday worship service back in town, they do commune by lunching together. One of them is named Cross. Finally, the hymn with which the action ends suggests that *Day*'s true subject consists of parts searching for oneness under the storm cloud of an approaching war.

Differences between *Day* and *Forty* also leap out. The more sober, good-natured *Day* covers less time, a few hours (except for a brief epilogue), as opposed to the sixty-eight years traced by its predecessor. Dialogue in *Day* is also less self-consciously brilliant. Operating from his home base of Yorkshire, Bennett feels more comfortable with his materials, not needing to embellish them with song parodies, sight gags, or allusions to earlier dramatists like Wilde and Brecht. This rejection of the high urban gloss of *Forty* is deliberate—and productive. Besides being written in a north-country dialect, *Day* has a greater social spread. It includes, among other figures, an industrial mogul, a socialist, some blue bloods and their gamekeeper, and three handicapped youngsters, each of whom has a different problem.

The action starts in May 1911 in Halifax, a mill town of dingy streets, slouching buildings, and grimy windows. The members of a local cycling club are meeting for a ride into the country. Their meeting place, the local war memorial, bodes ill for the expedition. How ill this foreboding is shows in the play's last scene, which also takes place at the war memorial, but in 1919. New names extend the list of war casualties engraved on the column, honoring local youths who died in World War I. But the storm cone and the havoc the war brings both pass, as the movie's last scene shows. Some survive the havoc, though without learning as much from it as they should. The idea that life goes on radiates much of the Bennett canon. Countervailing the commonness of the idea is the astuteness that goes into its treatment. This astuteness suffuses most of the frames of *A Day Out,* a work that answers to Bennett's description of a Thomas Hardy poem: "an incident, no moral drawn" (*PM* 10).

III

The opening of the 1984 movie *A Private Function* recalls *Forty Years On.* But rather than including an interior play, it opens with a newsreel that surveys conditions in Britain. The newsreel reports events all too familiar to those watching them in the cinema hall. November 1947 was a time of severe shortages in food, fuel, and electricity. The austerities brought about by these shortages created a thriving black market along with a

SOME USES OF HISTORY

mood of national depression. Adapted from a short story by Bennett and Malcolm Mowbray, *Function* takes a dry-eyed look at a time of crime and suffering remembered by few, mostly because of the vividness of the war preceding it. More memorable to the Britons who lived through their country's postwar hardships was the wedding, later in the month, of Princess Elizabeth and Lieutenant Philip Mountbatten. *Function* carries forward *A Day Out*'s interest in bicycles, the chief mode of private local transport for Britons during the years of postwar reconstruction. Again like *Day*, *Function* calls for an acting style that features the ensemble; no one character in *Function* holds center stage for long spells at the expense of the others. Finally, like *Day*, the film concerns itself with power in a limited setting. This motif could stem from novels like C. P. Snow's *The Masters* (1954) and *The Conscience of the Rich* (1958), which came out during the early years of Bennett's intellectual growth. In *Function*, the car symbolizes power. A rich, influential local doctor, Charles Swaby, owns a car that keeps threatening the safety of Gilbert Chilvers, a chiropodist trying to build a practice.

The play's vectors of power converge on Gilbert. Having no clinic of his own, he cycles to his patients' homes, an arrangement that sometimes recoils on him. He's called a "nancy" (*PF* 89) and a "tapeworm" (*PF* 98). Some powerful locals stop him from renting the storefront where he wants to set up his clinic. But this "pleasant, mild-looking man in his thirties" (*PF* 19) maintains cheer. He converts part of his home into a clinic. He removes a nail from the foot of a pig named Betty. Later, he rescues the unlicensed pig from the farm where she is being kept until her owners see fit to butcher her. This man of goodwill extends the same regard to people. Despite being rebuffed, he keeps making friendly overtures to his neighbors. Moreover, women (and Bennett's women are usually more intuitive than his men) like Gilbert. One asks why he is not wearing his wedding ring, perhaps hoping that his marriage has come apart, which would free him for her. Gilbert's wife, Joyce, plans to keep him at home, though. There may be times when he wishes it were otherwise. Called in Bennett's introduction to the script "a distant relative of Lady Macbeth" (*PF* 8), this nerve-raked woman who refuses to have children wears herself out keeping busy. Besides looking after her mother, whom she treats as a surrogate child, she plays the organ in a local movie house and gives piano lessons. She also has social aspirations, serving drinks while clad in her finery to a group of leading local citizens who visit the Chilvers home unexpectedly.

What could tarnish the hopes of this self-dramatizing devotee of suffering is the identity of her possible deliverer. Bennett has plenty of good reasons to call Dr. Charles Swaby "a thoroughgoing shit" (*PF* 22) in his notes to the director. This rich, self-centered bully is greedy, careless, and indifferent to others. In one of his earliest speeches, he betrays a professional confidence. His careless, discourteous driving shows him abusing at a different level the power bestowed on him by his job. While at the wheel of his roadster, he sends Gilbert sprawling three times and mangles his bike. But Swaby is repeatedly pelted by garbage—the kitchen waste Gilbert collects to feed Betty the pig—a motif that imbues the plot with a pleasing note of Chaplinesque justice, the bully punctured. The garbage festooning the shoulders of Swaby, the Denholm Elliott role, may also represent a foreshadowing. It is no accident that Gilbert is such a frequent victim of Swaby's bad driving. The doctor wants to get rid of Gilbert, a fellow healer and thus a business rival. In fact, it is Swaby who blocks Gilbert from leasing clinic space on the town's busiest street.

Henry Allardyce, the estate agent who does Swaby's dirty work, is the odd man out in the three-man black-market-pork scheme along with Swaby and the "sour and small-minded" (*PF* 22) solicitor Frank Lockwood. Though despised by his two partners, Allardyce keeps a good heart. He loves Betty, whereas his cronies see her only as an investment. Now Bennett, a lover of animals, approves of others like him. The film's closing scene shows Allardyce and Gilbert fondling the "chubby pink" (*PF* 109) piglet they are feeding in an old railway wagon. Because of their common love of pigs, the two men have become friends. Their friendship, moreover, may lift Joyce and Gilbert Chilvers into the ranks of the town's social elite. But at how high a cost? And for how long? *Function* ends on a strident note. Perhaps the film's title takes its meaning from the final scene. But that meaning is hardly bright and hopeful. The piglet being fed and fondled is probably illegal in view of the tight controls imposed by the Ministry of Food. Could the piglet symbolize a thriving black market in pork, an activity hurtful to England's economy and morale? At risk, too, is Gilbert's marriage. The chiropodist is last seen with Allardyce and the piglet, not with Joyce. When Joyce (who is played by Maggie Smith) last appears on screen, she is dancing with Swaby at the Royal Wedding Dinner, where, coincidentally, pork is being served. Two sexual romps have just concluded: Joyce has managed to lure Gilbert into bed, and the boardinghouse proprietress, Mrs. Forbes, achieves her long-standing wish to have sex with her roomer, Ministry of Food inspector Maurice Wormold.

This arrangement suits Wormold, too. Though foiled in his quest for the black marketeers, he wins a bigger prize—the love of his landlady. He scores a hidden victory as well. Wormold does not know that Doris Forbes's long-term lover has been Douglas Nuttall (played by Pete Postlethwaite), an illegal traf-ficker in pork. If the self-denying, work-ridden inspector does not catch the crook, at least he steals the crook's woman. Justice has been served, however roughly. The equation of sex and food also emerges in the last scenes in a pattern underscored by the Forbes-Wormold bond. The locals' plan to kill Betty the pig moves forward in phase with the preparations for the Royal Wedding Dinner. A previous scene (*PF* 103), in fact, depicted a discussion of the royal wedding and honeymoon while a pig was being slaughtered in the next room. Then Doris Forbes browns her legs with gravy to simulate the look of nylons to tempt Wormold. Entering the unsuspecting Wormold's room, she hands him an eyebrow pencil, which he is to use to draw stock-ing seams along the backs of her legs, starting at the ankles and working up.

Swaby would leap at the chance to join the sex-food equa-tion. As was previously mentioned, he nearly crashed into Gil-bert three times with his car in the span of a day, and he did destroy Gilbert's bike. Then he stopped Gilbert from opening a clinic on the Parade. But he wants more: he is so incensed that he says he would like to crucify Gilbert (*PF* 96). He may have to settle for an affair with Gilbert's wife, chances for which look good. Leaving her the last time they meet before the wedding dinner, Swaby says, "you've gone up in my estimation. You've got more about you than your husband" (*PF* 106). Joyce did not protest this slight to Gilbert. Similarly, while dancing with Swaby near the end of the movie, she permits his hand to wander.

Any affair that develops between Joyce and Swaby faces hurdles. Relationships are convoluted in the closely knit small town in which *Function* unfolds. For example, Gilbert is Mrs. Allardyce's chiropodist, and Joyce gives piano lessons to the Allardyces' daughter, Veronica. As was discussed earlier, the meat inspector, Wormold, boards with a woman whose lover deals in black-market meat. Whatever dark meanings the action invokes, though, get hidden in the fun. Bennett keeps things moving, shifting scenes, introducing new characters, and bouncing the different subplots off of each other. Heating the action are a couple of police raids, traffic mishaps, and the abduction of Betty. Bennett's deft timing also declares itself in *Function*. While the Chilverses are looking for a way to kill Betty, their doorbell rings twice. Veronica Allardyce has come for her lesson, and then Wormold shows up to have Gilbert examine his feet. Wormold's unexpected appearance sounds a note of alarm, but only briefly. Betty has an attack of diarrhea minutes before Wormold's arrival, but his having German measles as a boy killed Wormold's sense of smell, keeping him from detecting the pig or her waste. Others, though, have picked up the stench, particularly Joyce's seventy-four-year-old incontinent mother, who fears that it comes from her.

The laughter provoked by this fun cannot negate the impression of wrongness rising from *Function*. That impression

calls to mind the disturbing biblical passage "Unto those who
have, it shall be given; unto those who have not, it shall be taken
away" (Matthew 13:12; Mark 4:25; Luke 8:18). Again, Bennett
makes the point through the medium of food. Whereas the crooks
Lockwood, Allardyce, and Swaby enjoy a rich steak dinner while
plotting to market their wares, the Chilverses eat modestly in
the next scene, and, minutes later, Wormold finishes a spartan
meal consisting of a "thin soup with two veg" (*PF* 38). This
inequity carries forward, ingraining itself as a staple of postwar
Britain. All the guests at the Royal Wedding Dinner are feasting
grandly, as is the wedding party a couple of hundred miles away
at Buckingham Palace—also on pork. Meanwhile, there is no
end in sight to the food shortage vexing the country. The bold-
ness of the image of a pig sticker flung onto a table "where it
sticks quivering" (*PF* 78) drives home the notion of harsh realities firmly in place. The image, which works better on the screen
than on the stage or television, shows style and subject working
together in *A Private Function,* Bennett developing the texture
of an obscure moment in British social history with his usual
verve and cunning.

IV

Like many of Bennett's other scripts, *Enjoy* finds its author
looking at both past and future and then showing how the ugliness of the previous decades forecasts an outlook as frightening
as it is grim. The 1980 play, an amalgam of black humor, family
drama, and social criticism, takes place in the last surviving home

in a neighborhood being demolished. The dilapidated building where Connie ("Mam") and Wilfred ("Dad") Craven, a couple in their sixties, live exudes exhaustion. Though Mam and Dad's living room is neat and looked after, Mam (played by Joan Plowright) has lost her memory, and Dad (played by Colin Blakely), whose eyesight has been failing, is paralyzed below the neck, the victim of a hit-and-run driver. The couple must strain to present a front of middle-class respectability. It soon becomes clear, as well, that Connie and Wilfred Craven are working hard to avoid conflict. Their conversation wheels around in tired circles, various topics of discussion crisscrossing and overlapping. But the dialogue is not as random as it sounds. Whenever a topic swerves into a danger zone, it is either suppressed or shunted to the side.

The frequency with which these topics surface keeps the Cravens on their guard. Mam's chief concern at the outset is looking respectable. "It's no crime, cleanliness" (*Plays One* 282), she says, voicing her fear of being scorned as low class. Recent developments have quickened this fear. She takes pride in occupying a corner house on a street once esteemed as elegant and chic. But now that the house is being razed as part of an urban renovation plan, she and Dad are moving into a public-accommodation flat, which her passion for respectability misleads her into calling a "maisonette" (*Plays One* 268). Reality has been thwarting this passion. She admits that her future neighbors sometimes piss in the elevator and that a baby was recently found in one of the waste-disposal chutes. She does not know that *maisonette* is a term for a love nest that urban businessmen

rent for their extramarital intrigues; no businessman of any standing would rent a unit in the cinder block sty where the Cravens
are being stowed.

Mam's worst nightmare, though, come from dealing with
Dad, who hates himself for having caved in to evil impulses,
not only because they are evil but also because society has always condemned them. Now he sits immobilized, this elder with
two grown children, wondering what form his punishment will
take. Lacking reserves, he is insecure, defensive, and easily un-
hinged. His having suffered from shingles (*Plays One* 284) bespeaks the nervous disorder that keeps driving to the surface of
his seemingly tranquil life. Disordered his nerves are. Without
provocation, a painful revelation painfully expressed will burst
into his conversation. For example, he tells a social worker,
apropos of nothing previously said, "I don't want to give you
the idea I'm trying to hide something, or that anything unortho-
dox goes on between my wife and me. It doesn't. Nothing goes
on. . . . No foreplay. No afterplay. And fuck all in between"
(*Plays One* 276–77). Yet later, while talking to Mam, he claims
that the social worker, who has kept silent since walking into
the Cravens' home, "wormed all sorts out of me" (*Plays One*
283) during Mam's absence. The worm metaphor tells all. Dad
is far more conflictive and self-destructive than he appears, many
of his tics and fidgets referring to an old guilt that could drive
him mad.

But—in a question stirred by several of Bennett's old men—
does this man who lives in constant fear of falling over the edge
deserve sympathy? An innocent remark provokes him to hit Mam.
In some way, Mam's "I know you do" (282), confirming his

claim that he loves their daughter, Linda, found a sore spot in the drama welling inside him. A way into this terrible drama comes in his oft-repeated request that Mam and then Linda feel his arm. Now useless and dead to sensation, the arm nonetheless reminds him of the power he enjoyed when he was in charge of six workers or, as he puts it, when "I had six men under me" (*Plays One* 266). The idea of sexual domination or control peppers his speech. Act 2 of *Enjoy* begins with his long disquisition on the phrase *no love lost* (*Plays One* 299). The phrase, he says, has always puzzled him. "Does it mean," he wonders, "that the love between the persons concerned was so precious that they could not bear to spill a single drop? And thus no love went to waste. Taking love as some kind of liquid. I'm thinking of me and Linda" (*Plays One* 299). No doubt the two subjects have merged in his mind in the form of incestuous desire (craving-Craven-cowardly). He says he would like to start a life alongside Linda, a life so pure and high-minded that it would bypass altogether the question of his spilling his seed inside of her.

He is lying. He has probably already forced Linda. His arm (which he always refers to in the singular) evokes for him his lost manhood. Perhaps by feeling it, Linda can restore its potency. He himself identifies the arm, along with his nearly sightless eyes, as "three erogenous zones" (*Plays One* 277) that have stopped working for him. The Oedipal association called forth by his bad eyes fits neatly with his view of his arm as a penis substitute. This view supports Linda's claim that he interfered with her (*Plays One* 327), a claim, by the way, he never denies. The liquid he associates with love refers to the sperm he wants to give Linda.

Perhaps he has already given it to her. Linda's behavior suggests the anger of an abused daughter. At the outset, it is said that she, an urbane, efficient private secretary, has accompanied her boss to a business conference in Sweden. The story is false. She has not gone anywhere, even though she soon makes it clear that she would rather be anywhere than in her parents' home. "Shit" (*Plays One* 28) is the first word she says after coming into the home, and she repeats it four times before saying anything else. She blames her outburst on the heel of her shoe, which has broken. Her early association with breakage and waste is deliberate. Linda is not a private secretary but rather a prostitute, and she probably broke the heel of her shoe walking the streets looking for customers. The streets are her element. A stranger to chic, she let herself be duped into believing that her Rumanian shoes were a bargain. "Made in Rumania," she insists; "You can't get better workmanship than that. They're Rumanian pigskin" (*Plays One* 284). Like Jean, Strindberg's lackey in *Miss Julia* (1888), Linda has mistaken Rumanian shoddiness for elegance. And like Lesley, the bit-part actress in *Her Big Chance,* from Bennett's *Talking Heads,* she is a pseudo-sophisticate who keeps getting gulled.

She hasn't been to Sweden (Strindberg's native land). But she is bound for more distant, as well as more exotic, climes. She is planning to fly to Arabia, where she is going to settle with the prince she will marry that very afternoon. Now even though she has only been on stage for ten minutes, she has made it clear that the marriage will never take place. Bennett convincingly builds a mood of skepticism. Although the prince has never met Linda, he has seen her picture, and he is sending a car to fetch her to the wedding. Her comment "Only the bugger's late" (*Plays One* 291) confirms the viewer's suspicions. Linda has wasted every lucky break she could have used to better herself. A tart she will remain. When the "handsome brute of a chauffeur" (*Plays One* 294) in charge of the limousine that is to take her to her prospective bridegroom pulls up to the Cravens' home and comes inside, he and Linda roll on the floor together in a wild embrace, even though they are probably strangers. This wildness enforces her pattern of defeating her best hopes. She and the chauffeur later leave the Craven home, but not to attend her wedding. When she comes back, not surprisingly with another man at her side, she explains that she was one of six finalists from a field of twenty-five women being auditioned by the prince's agent, a man from Lloyd's Bank. "[A]lthough I'd done very well on the oral examination my tits fell short of the standard required" (*Plays One* 313), she cites as the banker's explanation for dropping her as a candidate.

She never does display the slow, easy serenity that goes with the maternal love she might have extended to her son Anthony. In fact, she resists love of all kinds. She refuses to kiss her parents goodbye before presumably setting off for Arabia, and she insults the chauffeur of the Arabian prince after mauling him on the floor. Bennett accounts for this coldness. "I don't want love. I want consumer goods," (*Plays One* 287), she tells her mother in act 1. Later, in a more painful self-disclosure, she says, "My problem is: I hate my loved ones" (*Plays One* 296). She has every reason to yoke love with hatred. Molested as a child, she knows firsthand the devastation that love can cause. Safer to be a prostitute or to indulge in casual sex. And if you tire of this

routine, marry a rich stranger. The trouble is that she cannot follow her own advice. Love keeps intruding. In spite of herself,
she still loves the father who abused her. And each denial of this
love gives her psyche another painful wrench. Her guilt-plagued
father worsens the pain. He makes every allowance for her and
keeps repeating that he both loves her and lives for her. When
Linda, attempting to flee her sordid past, denies her parentage,
he insists on his paternity, but he does so with a metaphor that
keeps it in the shadow of sex: "I'm the genuine parent. No question. But when it comes to who her mother was I'm a bit stumped"
(*Plays One* 289). This university graduate in philosophy has lost
his power both to reason and to express himself without giving
offense. His lapse grabs Linda's attention. She has become a
hooker to punish him. Her line of work mocks both the love he
keeps lavishing on her and the middle-class morality he has always claimed to uphold.

But Linda is not his only child. Are he and his long-absent
son Terry joined by a truth uglier than the incest he forced on
Linda, though? And who is Terry, anyway? And why does his
centricity in the Craven family take so long to surface? In a diary entry written while *Enjoy* was previewing in Richmond,
Bennett said of the play that its "central character is in drag
throughout" (*WH* 109). What makes Bennett's cross-dressing
Terry Craven so central is his grip on his parents' psyches. Early
in the action, those parents have the following conversation:

DAD: He'll not come.
MAM: Who?
DAD: I won't say his name . . .

SOME USES OF HISTORY

> MAM: I wonder if he's famous: he went to London.
> DAD: Yes, we know what for.
> MAM: Its institutions and libraries. It's public buildings, the concerts, art galleries and places of interest.
> DAD: Not forgetting its superb toilet facilities. . . . Purlieus of that nature. Talking of love. (*Plays One* 270)

The toilets to which Dad is referring are gay pick-up places. Even though he refuses to mention his son by name, he does detail what he condemns as his son's great failing. This odd fusion of detail and vagueness shows that, in Terry, the Cravens are discussing a red-hot subject. That subject, along with the guilt it has inflicted upon Mam and Dad, keeps recurring. A minute or so after he is discussed by them, Terry knocks on his parents' door. A social worker, he now calls himself Terri, or Kim, Craig and dresses as a woman. The local council has sent Ms. Craig to observe the Cravens. Her findings will help the council preserve both their sense of identity and the traditional community values that the old back-to-backs helped shape. Ms. Craig will say nothing during her visit. Rather than performing for her benefit, the Cravens must remain oblivious of her, acting as they would if alone together in the house.

But her silence cows them and throws them off stride, as does her person. Mam and Dad may have even recognized Terry as soon as he walked in, which may have been his intention; he has come to his parents in high drag to show them one of the effects of their mistreatment of him. Even before he enters the house as Ms. Craig, Dad said, "She's come to kill me" (*Plays One* 272). It is irrelevant that his near-blindness clouds his perception of Ms. Craig. He knows that retribution awaits him, and he also suspects the form it will take—the female role he forced on Terry when molesting him. Dad even seems to invite retribution. Ms. Craig is in the house less than two minutes before he tells her that he and Mam have only one child, a daughter. No sooner does Mam refer to a second child than he sends her into the kitchen to make tea. And once she is gone, he presents his arm to Ms. Craig, but he does so in terms much more aggressive than any he uses with either Linda or Mam: "Grip it. Go on. Grip it hard. Listen, I'm old enough to be your father. . . . Bite it. Go on. Bite the bugger" (*Plays One* 277).

Perhaps Dad means that Ms. Craig should grip and then bite his arm because he *is* Ms. Craig's father. Presumably subversive, such behavior between parent and child is normal in the home. It may even have precedents. Dad tells Mam that he caught their son at age fifteen wearing one of her frocks. But he doesn't describe his reactions to the discovery, which might have been uglier than his misconduct with Linda. Late in the second act, Dad accuses Terry of wanting him dead. Then, gorged with guilt, he asks Terry to kill him. Terry follows his own response to Dad's request, "I don't want to kill you" (*Plays One* 331), with a goodbye hug and kiss despite Dad's protests. Having forced Dad into the submissive female posture, he has done enough. If he wanted to avenge himself on an abusive father, he has succeeded brilliantly.

Dad will have to live the dregs of his life in a hospital, where he will have plenty of time to brood on his sins. In fact, he will be free to brood without distraction, since he can expect few or no visitors. Terry would have done his father a favor by killing

him. He can exact a sharper revenge by subjecting Dad to the
rigors of being alone and forgotten. Though the play includes no
evidence linking Terry to the hit-and-run incident that immobilized Dad, the event prefigures the less spectacular but more
vexing fate of Dad's having only his guilt and shame to keep
him company. But at least he will be safe from attacks by immediate family members, just as they will be safe from him. "The
home is more dangerous than the roads apparently" (*Plays One*
315), says a minor figure. The dysfunctional Craven home vin-
dicates this judgment. The Cravens' wedding site, a church since
converted into a discount warehouse (*Plays One* 289), implies
the corruption of love by market values.

As was noted earlier, Linda prefers consumer goods to love.
She would also like to change parents. She is out of phase with
the realities of her life. If he is her son, Anthony has turned from
her as ruthlessly as she did from Mam and Dad. Family members reject or deny each other in *Enjoy*. Besides gainsaying the
existence of Terry, Dad disowns his tie with Anthony, who comes
into the house calling him Grandad. Though no blood tie between the two can be inferred, Anthony does know that Dad has
a steel plate in his head; he recognizes Linda's picture in a magazine; and he is unique in calling Dad "Wilfred." Then he nearly
kills Dad by smashing him in the head. What's more, Terry/Ms.
Craig lets Anthony into the Cravens' home. Violence has perhaps once again impinged on the blood tie, with Terry/Ms. Craig
orchestrating the process from the wings. He has done enough.
The enemy in Bennett's play, though, is not a parent but a grand-
parent, a forebear on which youngsters can usually lean to relieve the harshness of parental justice. Knowing that Dad will

extend him no kindness or mercy, Anthony strikes out. Nor is his violence shocking. An enemy of love herself, Linda never taught Anthony how to be kind and gentle, making him feel deprived. His deprivation worsened because of Dad's refusal to ease it.

The consequence of this refusal obeys a logic long in place: damaged people damage others, most often those who have damaged *them*. This damage symbolizes the downfall of the nuclear family as we know it. Just as Ms. Craig enters the Cravens' home as an observer, so does Anthony have at *his* side a young man carrying a notebook. Like Third World primitives, the Cravens come before the audience accompanied by social scientists. Perhaps the council that assigned Ms. Craig and Gregory to the Cravens wants to document the collapse of the basic two-child family and, with it, the middle class. These two bulwarks of the industrial West have been imploding. Linda's denial of her lineage in favor of commodities expresses itself in the name of the chauffeur she gropes and claws at their first meeting, Heritage. Perhaps her rolling together on the floor with Heritage signals the emergence of a new order, a rough beast much colder and grittier than the prevailing one. Perhaps the new order has already begun. And nobody deserves to inaugurate it any more than the self-defeating Linda.

An answer to this question comes in the way names are used in the play. As was mentioned earlier, Anthony smashes Wilfred after calling him by name. He also refers directly to Linda after seeing her nude photo in a girlie magazine. Anthony shows Dad the photo to torment him, asking, "Those tits ring a bell?" (*Plays One* 304). They may ring a bell with Anthony himself. Her breasts foiled her bid to marry the Arabian prince: the banker who inspected them found them "a bit on the old side" (*Plays One* 313), Linda explains. Perhaps Anthony will repay her maternal neglect of him by striking out at her as he did at her father, the other person in the play he calls by name. Near the end, Ms. Craig calls Mam "Connie," a practice to which Dad objects not because naming a person implies an intent to inflict harm but because Ms. Craig withholds the same grace from him. He is angry and hurt. Since a name confers identity, the omission or avoidance of naming a person during conversation amounts to a denial of the person. Mam affirms her acceptance of Ms. Craig by calling her Kim. And when Dad tries to persuade the social worker to take him with her, he says that he, too, will call her Kim. Ms. Craig's rejection of his plea shows Bennett's irony working at two levels. She knows all too well the dangers that could burst from the kind of family circle Dad has invoked by saying the name *Kim*. Families can maim and bruise. To protect herself from these depredations, she bids Dad goodbye.

What she walks into is a world without guidelines. This world is so deracinated that it blurs boundaries between men and women and even between life and death. After being cudgeled, Dad seems to be dead; a neighbor is "ninety-nine per cent sure" (*Plays One* 307) that Anthony killed him. While being readied for the coffin, though, Dad gets an erection. He is alive, after all. But this rising proves misleading. His resurrection is dim and feeble. Incontinent, he wets himself rather than producing the sperm that would mark a return to manhood. He also gains his wish of having his arm not only stroked but rather massaged. This attention comes, though, from a Mr. Harmon, director of the urban renewal project that has relegated Dad to a hospital for the infirm. Dad might have preferred death to the loneliness and sorrow that await him as he lies incontinent and paralyzed in a bleak place where he is a stranger. Yet no family member will help him. His erection, however brief, makes him a potential danger to any intimate.

The world he is leaving, even though he helped form it, is so brutal and denatured that survival in it calls for a disguise. Any of its inhabitants who use their real names or walk around without masks will meet grief. Perhaps the person called Ms. Craig can give the others a lesson in coping. Linda says of her, "He obviously fancies me. How can he be a nancy?" (*Plays One* 328). Linda's reaction to meeting Ms. Craig, "I find him not unattractive" (*Plays One* 326), suggests that she has projected her own erotic feelings onto her parents' visitor. But this self-projection is natural. Neither Craven child should shrink from incest; they have both known it from childhood. As in Shelagh Delaney's *Taste of Honey* (1958), life in *Enjoy* is so rancid that the characters feel obliged to savor the rare moments of fun that await them, regardless of the cost.

Terry wields his self-protective irony amid shadows and recesses. Appreciating historical continuity, local urban redevelopers plan to dismantle and then rebuild the Cravens' back-to-back in a museum situated in a theme park dedicated to preserving tradition. The council heads believe that they are enshrining the values of neighborhood, family, and home to ward off rampant change. Mam, who becomes the home's sole occupant, will transmogrify into a museum exhibit, fulfilling the council's aim of preserving social stability and continuity. Like Sam Shepard's

True West (1980), *Enjoy* questions the practice of celebrating values that may have never existed. Yes, the old back-to-back row houses that for decades supported life in cities like Leeds had a coziness and warmth. The relocation of the Cravens' home to a museum stands as a tribute to this flinty charm, which evokes meals of tripe, cowheel, and trotters cooked on a coal fire. But the smoke rising from these flames summons up the inconvenience, backwardness, and squalor of daily life in pre-1950 Leeds. Imposing this grubbiness on the freakishness of Anthony's generation leaves little to celebrate. The legacy of belonging transmitted by the working-class English family amounts to a dance of death.

Though grim and grotty, this dance engages the spirits. "A most successful play," said Thomas E. Luddy in his review of *Enjoy.*[6] As Luddy shows, superior direction, acting, and staging can help the play succeed. Puzzling and irreverent as it is, it need not sink into ponderousness. Bennett enhances its snappy dialogue with his usual grasp of the visual and auditory resources of the stage. *Enjoy* both challenges and provides a feast for the senses. In act 2, Mam and Ms. Craig begin dancing "in great style" (*Plays One* 315) for no apparent reason. Later in the act, the museum's projects director inspects the Cravens' mantelpiece, curtains, wallpaper, and bath. Then Bennett reveals the reason behind the inspection; a crew comes onstage to dismantle the home and to cart away the walls and furniture. The end of the play shows Dad, Mam, and Ms. Craig addressing each other across an empty stage.

As riveting as the play's dialogue is, the biggest gains reaped by *Enjoy* stem from Bennett's ability to make the uncanny look ordinary and the ordinary seem opaque. In the Cravens' sorry back-to-back, he evokes a time, a place, and a mood, thanks partly to a sure touch with details that lends the play a nightmarish concreteness. The Bennett of *Enjoy* stands far from the polite, understated purveyor of nuances for which he is usually taken. By combining naturalism with surrealism and the sinister with the coarse,[7] he has created a touching, moving, involving play out of bleak, unforgiving materials. *Enjoy* is strong stuff, but it is honest stuff. Both the vision and the craft that went into it, though adding little to Bennett's popularity, shore up his status as one of England's best living playwrights.

V

The Madness of George III (1991) combines erudition, common sense, and elegance. Its depth and rigor have also deservedly made it both Bennett's most acclaimed stage play and the inspiration for the 1994 film *The Madness of King George,* recipient of three Academy Award nominations and, for now, the only one of Bennett's works with which he is identified in the United States. Judgments about his title figure range as wide as those on any other topic in the field of historical research, and the former Oxford historian Bennett hazards no startling breakthroughs. Rather than faulting George or any of his biographers, he accepts the truth that history is always contested.

John Lahr's October 1993 review of the play in the *New Yorker* opens with the statement "Alan Bennett's 'The Madness of George III' begins just after the monarch loses the colonies and just before he loses his mind."[8] Bennett does invite a tie-in between the two events. The colonies of which Lahr speaks are the American colonies, a development that the members of the royal court avoid mentioning in George's presence. Would that George himself were so tactful. Not only does he keep referring to the loss of the colonies, but he also foresees both the independence of India and the collapse of the empire—during his reign. Such dread imaginings could easily bedevil a monarch. But so could porphyria, a metabolic disorder that addles its victims' minds while turning their urine purple or blue. Bennett keeps alive the possibility that George suffered from porphyria. Besides discussing the idea in the play's introduction (*MGIII* viii–ix), he has his characters refer several times to the blueness of the royal water.

But George's recovery of his wits includes a new balance of understanding. As he says near the end of the play, every life has its consolations as well as its regrets. And many of the consolations that have graced him come from his person rather than his office. He has enjoyed twenty-eight happy years of marriage to Charlotte, a sign of which is the brood of fifteen children they have had together. And even though Charlotte has always been homely, he has remained faithful to her. His fidelity shows that he is a man of broader sensibilities and more enduring values than has often been credited. Bennett himself speaks of George's "attachment to his people and his vision of the nation over and above the vagaries of politics" (*MGIII* viii). George's behavior in the play validates this judgment. An active, hands-on sovereign, he knows astronomy and animal husbandry, and he has kept abreast of developments in both industry and farming. His subjects call this author of several treatises on architecture

"Farmer George" (*MGIII* 2). And, besides reminding a house-hold maid that the coal she thought grew in the castle's cellar came from quarries in Wales, he researches the political and family backgrounds of each of his prospective appointments.

Bennett judged well in 1995 to call the king "conscientious and well-informed."[9] Bennett also showed artistic wisdom in giving George a life away from the throne. George's speech has a poetic ring, as is seen in his musings about America: "I had an empire once. There were forests there and lakes and plains and little soft hills" (*MGIII* 49). He continues his indulgent ways. Flouting his doctor's instructions to take three spoonfuls of a mild purgative, he knocks back two full glasses and then acts shocked when the fourteen bowel movements that ensue "could have manured the whole parish" (*MGIII* 10). His wit is not always so keen. Though benevolent, Bennett's George guards his royal prerogatives. In fact, his insistence on preserving the honors attending the throne has lent the court a stifling rigor. Speaking from a soft chair, he denies a heavily pregnant member of the royal retinue the comfort of sitting down during an orchestral concert.

George sticks to royal protocol even when doing so can hurt him. Anyone leaving the regal presence must walk backwards, always facing the king. To be caught looking at George or questioning him directly also counts as impertinence, including cases where the would-be questioner is his doctor. The royal physician explains the woes that beset him whenever the king is sick: "I cannot address His Majesty until he addresses me. I cannot enquire after His Majesty's symptoms until he chooses to inform me of them" (*MGIII* 9). Such recitations seduce the audi-

ence into feeling superior, but not for long. The etiquette ruling
George's court creates a world vastly different from ours, one
not answerable to the standards and guidelines of today. Thus
the decision on the part of his keepers to interrupt him or to tie
him up goes beyond the suspension of protocol. These actions
violate traditions and taboos long in place. They amount to a
desecration, yet one mandated to restore the hegemony of the
crown. The person of the king must be brought back into line
with the regal office. George has caused a dire problem; in his
madness, he has besmirched the honor and dignity of the throne.
Because all appointments flow from him, his incapacity has
brought the business of government to a standstill.

Madness was written from a conservative standpoint consistent with the politics of its 1788 time setting. Since the continuance of the state depends on the king's recovery, a long illness
could threaten the throne itself; the more protracted the royal
illness, the more difficult it will be to hide from the public. And
the commonweal must remain the chief concern of any government. "An ailing King means an ailing Government," intones
William Pitt, George's prime minister (*MGIII* 21). But other
misfortunes will take place that endorse Sophocles's equation
of the well-being of any nation with that of its leader. The London stock market plunges, the economy staggers, and normal
family relationships invert. Bennett attends closely to this viola-
tion of the natural order. "No, no. This must not be, the son in
charge of the father," says Queen Charlotte in the movie version
of the play.[10]

The play accepted the Freudian and Sophoclean offshoots
of the son's political ambitions. The Prince of Wales wants to

drive George from the throne and be declared regent. Distorting the historical record for the sake of dramatic punch, Bennett portrays Prin's eagerness to usurp his father's powers in terms that make George fear that his son wants to bed Charlotte. "The fat hands. That young belly. Those plump thighs. The harlot's delight" (*MGIII* 28), babbles the king, tormenting himself as he imagines a disorder both political and domestic. Government is as much a function of housekeeping in *Madness* as it was in *Oedipus*. As long as the royal family is disordered, the state will droop. And disorder inflames the king's worst fears. The Prince of Wales denies George access to Charlotte, a step Prin would take if he wanted her for himself.

The tie-in with *Hamlet* occurred to Bennett, as it should; as England's sovereign, George represents the line of dynastic succession as well as the nation. Bennett defines the succession in terms less political than literary. That George imagines into life an incestuous love triangle involving himself, his son, and his wife is riveting because of the chord it strikes with its Shakespearean and Sophoclean forebears. The chord reverberates. By invoking Hamlet's teasing of Polonius in act 3, scene 2, of Shakespeare's play, the king's statement in the film "I once saw a sheep with five legs" (*MKG* 70) tells the devotee of drama that George has recovered his wits; his madness has become methodical. But most of the way, the king is more pathetic than he is witty. Bennett positions him with one of his pages to remind the playgoer of Lear and the Fool. The comparison with Lear is important. George's many heartfelt references to his dead son Octavius call to mind Lear's memories of Cordelia. George has already made the identification. He directs, casts, and acts in the passage from *King Lear* (act 4, scene 7) that dominates the next-to-last scene of *Madness.* George's choice of the passage signals his readiness to assume the throne. It includes reminders of some of his worst moments, which occurred, Lear-like, when he was lucid. The knowledge that he had become an obscene blasphemer unable to suppress the filth spewing from him had made him hateful to himself.

Facing that hatred helps him move on. His self-disgust also bespeaks the art with which Bennett manipulates audience reaction throughout. George gains audience sympathy early because of his gentleness with his would-be assassin. Mrs. Nicholson had sought an audience with him; in her opinion, the Crown had stolen some of her land, and she wants redress. In her anger, she stabs the king. Bennett need not judge the merits of her plea. The purpose of the stabbing scene is to show George extending mercy to an attacker; he does not want Mrs. Nicholson hurt. First seen with his wife, this champion of the virtues of family, home, and domestic routine also lets his retainers know that Mrs. Nicholson's knife has not harmed him.

What helps win him added sympathy is the ruthlessness with which his son tries to depose him. Even if George were to recover his wits after the regency was established, no one would know. Prin would have kept George under house arrest in some remote hideaway from which reports about his health could be screened carefully before reaching the public. But Prin is not always on stage trying to score off his father. Bennett also gains favor for George by conveying the royal madness linguistically. Unable to control his speech, George either repeats a word over and over or chatters nonstop, sometimes for four hours at a time.

His entrapment in a cage of language takes different forms. Invoking his royal privilege, he balks at playing object to his doctor's subject; as king, he has always incited action rather than being ruled by a verb chosen by another noun subject. As long as he remains subordinate, he forfeits control, sometimes being relegated in his mind to a subordinate clause (*MGIII* 32). The fetters tighten on him. He calls the restraining chair into which he is forced at the end of part 1 "a fastening chair, a fasten-in chair, a fashioning chair to fashion the King to the ordinary fashion" (*MGIII* 48).

George has always preferred freedom. When he ordained that his assailant Mrs. Nicholson be spared from torture in the play's first scene, he said, "The lowliest subject in this kingdom could not be subjected to . . . tortures in the name of justice" (*MGIII* 30). Ironically, this sparer of a would-be killer from torture faces torture himself, but for a cause just as vital as justice—the preservation of the state. His wailing about "doctors, doctortures, doctormentors, doctalk" (*MGIII* 37) conveys his progressive retreat into language. His reserves fail him most often in the presence of sex. Suspecting or fearing that the twenty-six-year-old Prin covets Charlotte along with the crown, he wrestles his son to the ground and starts choking him. Earlier, the king had kissed Charlotte's lady-in-waiting, the beautiful Elizabeth Pembroke, "full on the lips" (*MGIII* 18), an insult all the more shocking for being perpetrated in front of his wife. Still more shock value comes from the recollection that, early in the play, Bennett established George's marital fidelity. George enters the play with Charlotte alongside him (in the movie, the whole family is at his side), and he claims, in the play's second scene, that his marriage has worked so well because he has always rated character over beauty (*MGIII* 5).

This good sense, which is buttressed by twenty-eight years of domestic harmony, recedes quickly because of the attention he keeps lavishing on Lady Pembroke in Charlotte's presence. At times, his degradation looks complete. "He soils his clothes. Urine. Excrement. He talks filth, the slops of his mind swilling over" (*MGIII* 35), says a royal equerry of George at his nadir. This assessment, painful in its accuracy, has both political and sexual import. In his madness, George uses a great deal of water imagery. He fears that his mania has split his body, allowing water to seep in. And as he takes in water, he sinks ever deeper into a whirlpool that threatens to close around him. Bennett carries the symbolism a step further, equating the waters that haunt George with the excreta and verbal swill that gush from him in place of the life-giving sperm that helped elevate him as both a patriarch and the father of his country. That Lady Pembroke has supplanted Charlotte in his thoughts during his dementia implies the great gulf between that dementia and the control he needs to run the country.

This control he recovers, and Bennett charts the recovery the same way as he did his dementia—through the medium of speech. George's idiosyncratic speech, once a sign of his eccentricity, signals his recovery when it resumes late in the play. George began his first two speeches in the play, both of which were one-liners, by saying "What, what" (*MGIII* 10). The restoration of these words to his conversation at the end shows his followers that he is once again normal, which for him means odd, since he was always that way. And odd he will stay, but perhaps to a lesser degree. His speech withal, his horrible ordeal may have helped him. Never a friend of dialectic, he always scorned any kind of opposition or resistance. But this aging, opinionated brat long accustomed to having his way has learned that being challenged can help both him and the state. The point is made by the Lincolnshire specialist in mental disorders who is called in to treat him: "To be curbed, stood up to, in a word thwarted, exercises the character, elasticates the spirit, makes it pliant. It is the want of such exercise that makes rulers rigid" (*MGIII* 40). Nearly immediately, George shows that being weaned from the deference and compliance he has always taken for granted humanizes him. He humbles himself by asking forgiveness from and kissing the hand of a servant he had wronged.

This humility promotes the moral balance he needs to rule effectively. As soon as this modesty asserts itself, the old knack snaps back into place. After reading *King Lear* with some associates, he says, "I have remembered how to seem" (*MGIII* 70). His epiphany promises well for his reign. A king must be prudent, cautious, and diplomatic. This imperative rests on a gift for make-believe. Pretense is essential for a head of state. The finale of *Madness* also suggests that the image of power, rather than power's exercise, satisfies any body politic. As often happens in Bennett, both everything and nothing have happened; the status quo has been restored. But the restoration has also disclosed the illusion undergirding both government and the leader-follower bond. The play's closing moments describe the process in action. With regal aloofness, George dismisses the Lincolnshire doctor who saw him through his illness and improved his kingly effectiveness. But both the dismissal and the high-handedness in which it is framed confirm the value of Dr. Willis's treatment. If the doctor's feelings have been hurt, he can nonetheless call his royal interlude a success. Nor will it take much time for the prospect of a £1,000 annuity to heal any wounds inflicted upon his ego.

Bennett's introduction to the film version of *Madness* grazes Shakespeare's famous metaphor from *As You Like It,* "All the world's a stage," in its confirmation of the importance of play-acting to any ruler: "Monarchy is performance and part of the King's illness consists of his growing inability to sustain that performance" (*MKG* xxi). The last scene of the film shows George telling the Prince of Wales both to smile and to wave at the crowds of people cheering the royal family just outside St. Paul's Cathedral. His words merit the prince's obedience. The royal family has appeared in public to give their well-wishers the impression of domestic harmony and happiness. Even if they rest on pretense, such shows of joyful union gladden the public heart and, in the process, discourage rebellion. They also underscore the idea, seen too in Jean Genet, that being takes precedence over doing and that surface counts more than depth in the upper reaches of government. Rather than defining himself in action, a monarch must master the art of looking happy while doing nothing. The prince's inactivity is better training for the throne than he realizes, and George does well to advise him to follow the royal example of blending with his role.

This example, Prin will learn, includes the acceptance of at least two ironies. George has long known the absurdity of the playacting that monarchy entails. Yet he also appreciates the folly of going public with his knowledge. A royal exposure of kingly rule as theatrics would panic his subjects. And even if the panic were quelled, lives might have been lost, and the crown might shift to a head less experienced, able, and shrewd. George knows his kingly duties, even though they are unwritten. Because the commonweal rests on pretense, he gladly plays the archpretender. As Plato and Kant have noted, nobody knows firsthand the reality underlying appearances. Donning his kingly mask and displaying it to his subjects shows George accepting life on its own terms. The benefits mount. Because the authority radiating from the crown comforts the public, the royal charade is therapeutic as well.

Even though Bennett distorted his motives to gain dramatic heightening (*MGIII* xiv), the Prince of Wales stands light-years away from this wisdom. He would have made a dreadful king had George drowned in his madness. He has no hobbies. He cares little about the country or its people. Lacking spirit, he either uses others to fight his battles or fights dirty. Even though George had refused to be treated by Prin's personal physician, Dr. Richard Warren, Prin forces Warren on the dazed king. The prince's motives do him little credit. As heir apparent, he stands to gain the most if his father is declared medically unfit. Had being ousted from the throne crushed George, his son would have acquiesced. Family values mean as little to him as does his country's welfare. To speed his way to the crown, he forbids his parents to see each other, an act undertaken to deepen George's gloom.

This cruelty may stem from sources not merely political. Though young, Prin has already lost much of his youthful grace to drink. In the film, his king-father revokes his marriage to the

Catholic Mrs. Maria Fitzherbert (who is absent from the play).
Both king-father and queen-mother chide the prince within five
minutes of the opening curtain for being too fat. They continue
to belabor his stoutness as if it were a moral failing. The subject
dogs him. "A fat lot you care" (*MGIII* 75), George says in response to his son's question about the royal health. Then Charlotte says of the prince, "He's still fat" (*MGIII* 75) during this
final depicted family get-together. Being constantly criticized
could well have angered Prin, particularly because, though the
criticism is relentless, it is also both fair and just. His office as
Prince of Wales impinges mightily on appearances. His parents'
carping words, though, could hardly encourage him to diet. Even
the playgoer is sick of hearing them. So often do they fly, in fact,
that one suspects them to be motivated by self-interest. George
knows that a fit, trim-figured Prince of Wales presents a healthier
image of the royal family than a bloated one. Yet he may also be
chipping away at his son's self-esteem to crush any delusions of
grandeur that might inspire him to vault himself onto the throne.

Less ambivalent in *Madness* is Bennett's scorn for doctors,
a bias also present in *Habeas Corpus* (1973) and *A Private Function* (1984). Lacking both imagination and compassion, each of
the doctors in charge of treating George insists on doing so differently. To remove the humors vexing the king, Dr. Warren recommends blistering—that is, the application of hot cups to the
king's flesh. Sir Lucas Pepys, displaying the same moral and
professional rectitude, examines the royal stool, devoting
Swiftian attention to color, shape, and quantity. George Baker,
who is both the king's private doctor and president of the Royal
College of Physicians, reads George's pulse to determine the

best way to bleed and to purge him. Is Baker trying to weaken George or cure him? The question is not idle. Perhaps he wants more than the thirty guineas he receives every time he examines the king. Ignoring the shakiness of Britain's economy, Baker has been using his insider's knowledge of George's health to make cash withdrawals that have started a run on the Bank of England. Once word leaks that the king's doctor has sold his securities, every other investor will follow suit. Baker's excuse for his jobbery, "I am a poor man. I have a family to think of" (*MGIII* 22), has such a false ring to it that it should be dismissed out of hand.

Baker's foil, Dr. Willis, the Lincolnshire pastor-physician who takes charge of George during the worst days of the royal illness, wins audience approval because he is confident without being arrogant. Though he admits that he has never encountered an illness like His Majesty's, he is sure he can cure it. What gives him an edge over his fellow doctors is his patience in getting to know the king. Baker, Pepys, and Warren all fear Willis because, as an outsider, he has no political agenda. As soon as he finishes tending to George, Willis will return home rather than trying to win favor at Windsor Castle. His three colleagues' fear and dislike of him strengthen his resolve to treat George in his own way. Resisting their interference, he holds his ground and continues to gather information about the royal psyche. He also looks the king in the eye, tells him when to eat, and orders him to purge his speech of filth at pains of being straitjacketed or clamped in his restraining chair. This strategy works. After sparing George from one of Warren's blistering cups, he sees that his power to shield the king from pain has also gained him the royal obedience. Willis's granting George permission to see the queen moments later helps further shape a system of rewards that speeds the king's recovery.

If it did speed the recovery: both the stage and screen versions of *Madness* include passages that disclaim the worth of Willis's efforts (*MGIII* 77; *MKG* 70). Other passages impart stridency as well. For example, deceit helps improve one's status in Windsor more than compassion. Double-dealing lifts Captain Fitzroy to the rank of colonel. Conversely, three of the king's most faithful servants are shown the door lest their continued service to George remind him of his former woes. All subserves the welfare of the state, the embodiment of which is the king. Like any other military operation, the protection of the king and his family creates casualties. Yet it also deserves the efforts of George's Tory backers.

At times, it looks as if these efforts will fall. Though emphasizing character over plot, the six-month time span of *Madness* generates a great deal of suspense. A month after hiring Willis to cure the king, Pitt sees no improvement. How much longer can he afford to trust Willis? Pressure keeps building. A majority of fifty in favor of keeping George on the throne shrinks to thirty and then to ten. Fortunately, George halts the skid himself. His prattle now discloses streaks of sanity, however rankling to his listeners, like Hamlet's words to Polonius or those of the eponym of Pirandello's *Henry IV* (1922) to his doctor. By the time Prin gains a majority in the House of Commons, the king has recovered his wits. The bill to create a regency can be burned or, better, diced by the razor with which George shaves himself in view of his detractors in the film to confirm his recovery.

George and his eldest son are but two of a flock of colorful figures who represent the complex mix of the English court in 1788–89. The behavior of these figures describes a world both intimate and historical. There is also passion and historical depth in Bennett's portrayal of the king, an achievement more fully realized in the film than in the stage version. In 1996, Bennett said that movies need faster pacing than do stage or television dramas.[11] The regency crisis must have stayed alive in Bennett's mind after the November 1991 stage production of *Madness,* because there is no other explanation for the movie's superiority to the play. Nearly every change that Bennett introduced into the film script proved helpful, starting with Lord Chancellor Thurlow's aggressive simile in the film's opening frames, "God, this place is as cold as a greyhound's nostril" (*MKG* 6).

Here and elsewhere, the mobility of the camera both helps focus issues more clearly and lends the issues thematic bite. The close-in shots that describe George's decline into a howling, beshitten wreck seize the moviegoer with a force unattainable on the stage. Then there are the additions to the original text. George breaks his daily round in the film's early going to play with a pig, an act that supports the important claim that his kingliness includes a passion for the earthy. The fleshing out of the regal personality was a major concern of the film's director, Nicholas Hytner. George's appearance at the end in public surrounded by his whole brood leaves the viewer with a strong visual impression consistent with Bennett's working concept of the monarch as patriarch.

Finally, George's status as monarch inspired Bennett to bolster his text with the Prince of Wales–Mrs. Fitzherbert subplot. George *is* being cavalier and harsh by nullifying Prin's marriage. But the swiftness of the king's response to his son's disclosure that he has married Mrs. Fitzherbert captures the toughness of the born ruler. George is back in charge, which is where he belongs, at least for the time being. And kings do not dither or dally. Both his decisiveness with his son and the counterpoint of motives (his favorite composer was Handel) incited by his madness invoke issues and ideas trenchant enough to justify Robert Brustein's view of Bennett as "an important epic playwright,"[12] even though the play enjoyed less box-office success on Broadway, where Brustein saw it, than it did on London's West End.

CHAPTER FOUR

Kafka and Other Office Drones

The smart, exhilarating group of plays by Bennett dealing with corporate bonds makes the disturbing point that the lifeline between most people is hostility. The hostility may even be self-directed. The Kafka of *Kafka's Dick* and *The Insurance Man* (both produced in 1986) loathes his name, his looks, and his oeuvre. Once in a while, this hostility gives way to indifference. But these instances are rare, out of the home as well as in. In a diary he kept during BBC-TV2's mounting of the production of *The Insurance Man,* Bennett explained that all corporate ties founder on the reefs of the server-servee relationship: "It is a feature of institutions that the permanent staff resent those for whose benefit the institutions exist."[1] Thus teachers grouse about their students, lawyers complain about their clients, and doctors gripe about patients. But, as is shown in *Green Forms* (1978), colleagues who get along most of the time also direct waves of fear and distrust at each other when they feel their job security under threat.

Just as every business tie is colored by personal likes and dislikes, so do official and personal bonds in Bennett interweave. As in Joyce's short story from *Dubliners,* "Counterparts," both the language and the social dynamics of the office invade the Phillips home in *One Fine Day* (1979). Though happy in his retirement, Arthur Dodsworth of *A Visit from Miss Prothero* (1978) feels crushed by the discovery that a billing system he spent four years perfecting has been scrapped since his retirement four months earlier. That Dodsworth hears the crushing news at home carries forward the argument, implicit in *Enjoy* (1980), that even though the home and the workplace both unleash dangers, the worst disasters break in the nest. The shaky loyalty-rivalry interplay can disclose both insecurity and nastiness at any time. Evoking the love-hate syndrome that both defines and corrupts all of Wilfred Craven's close bonds in *Enjoy,* Hermann Kafka, the author's merchant father, and Max Brod, his literary executor and biographer, both take pride in the knowledge that one of the century's great writers owes his fame to them.

They cannot feel much pride. They owe as much to Kafka (1883–1924) as he does to them. Only his remarkable fiction has preserved their names. And since that fiction is Kafka's main legacy, Brod and Hermann know that, in the eyes of some, they survive as satellites or even parasites. Nor can they find solace in the agent of their survival; an effect cannot have more reality than its cause. The Kafka of *Kafka's Dick* feels unwanted, uncomfortable, and checked at every turn. Though his real-life model had a home, a fiancée, and a full-time job much of his adult life, he fit nowhere, this German-speaking Czech who was neither Christian nor Jew (*Kafka* xxvi). It is this nonbelonger we'll look at before spending time with his public self, the bureaucrat employed by Prague's Worker Accident Insurance Institute.

I

Geniuses have always irritated both their intimates and their survivors. When the genius disclaims his prominence, as Kafka did, the irritations mount. Bennett's 1986 screenplay of John

Lahr's biography of English playwright Joe Orton, *Prick up Your Ears,* compared the plight of Kenneth Halliwell, Orton's lover and eventual murderer, to that of the wife (and later widow) of a great man. Nudged into the shadows by her genius husband, she still has to protect him from fans, bill collectors, and talk-show hosts so that he has the freedom to exercise his genius. Nor can she tally the bouts of moodiness, temper tantrums, and drunken outbursts she had to put up with before his brilliant work reached its audience, a work that might never have been created at all without her years of forbearance. Obviously, it is the rare wife who feels adequately repaid or appreciated. In most cases, wifely sacrifice is forgotten or mocked. Thus Halliwell murdered Orton in 1967.

Max Brod did not take out his grievances against Kafka so dramatically, but then he would not have, since his tie with Kafka was asexual. Emotions only flared up after Kafka's death. During their years together in Prague, the hunchback Brod enjoyed more literary acclaim than his friend Kafka. He is still acclaimed, but not for the eighty-odd books he wrote during his long life (1884–1968). He owes his fame to his friend. Brod wrote Kafka's biography and edited a nine-volume edition of his unpublished fiction, diaries, and letters, in the process becoming the world's leading expert on his former friend. "But for me there would have been no Kafka," he says rightly (and righteously) in *Kafka's Dick;* "I made Kafka" (*Kafka* 18). Were it not for Brod, the 15,000 studies (*Kafka* ix) Kafka has inspired would never have been written. But Kafka would not have thanked Brod for making him famous. Fame touched Kafka because Brod disobeyed the author's dying wish to destroy all his unpublished writing.

KAFKA AND OTHER OFFICE DRONES

Brod's disobedience accounts for much of the fun in act 1 of *Kafka's Dick.* He and Kafka have both come back to life at the home of a middle-class English couple, Sydney and Linda. But Kafka, having predeceased his friend, does not know that Brod saw his literary remains into print. Wanting to preserve Kafka's ignorance, Brod convinces their host that they must avoid all discussion of the work, a hard job because Sydney's bookcase teems with books both on and by Kafka. Elements of farce carry the scene forward as some of the books that Sydney and Brod remove from the case spill to the floor, not always before Kafka catches sight of them. Then Linda revives the comic tension Bennett had previously relaxed, returning to the living room a stack of books Brod and Sydney had put in a hallway out of Kafka's view. Kafka's piecemeal discovery of his fame rankles him. In self-defense, Brod scorns what he sees as Kafka's ingratitude; anyone else would welcome the eminence that came from Brod's labors. Yet Brod also feels some guilt for having disobeyed Kafka; shortsighted and self-indulgent as it was, the dying request came from Kafka's heart and deserved to be honored for that reason. Brod's guilt has deepened over the years. Though Kafka owes his immortality to Brod, it is an immortality he never wanted. Besides, it diminishes Brod. Whatever reputation he has today comes from Kafka. He has become immortalized by an immortal who fought his immortality.

This chafing truth applies more strictly to Hermann Kafka (1852–1931), the writer's tyrannical father. Posterity has damned Hermann for having inflicted misery on his son. One can see why. He bullied and mocked Franz, hid his ink, and, at times, made love so noisily in the family's Prague apartment that he distracted Franz from writing his stories. But Bennett sees in this behavior more than the classic parental aggression that blocks the child's freedom. Calling Hermann one of the many "Parents of Art" (*Kafka* xiii) in his introduction to the two Kafka plays, Bennett extends the fancy-goods merchant some sympathy. Abusive fathers who warp their children also send them deep into their psyches, where the creative imagination has its home. Such fathers thus create their children twice, as people and then as artists. In an irony that Bennett could only relish, tyranny like Hermann's has gained the world some beautiful artifacts. It is irrelevant that these gains spoiled both the digestion and the sleep of the artists. Artists' well-being has always existed inversely with their artistry; all artists are battlefields. The number of paintings, sonatas, and novels that would have been lost had their creators been reared smiling and cooing is incalculable. Bad fathers enrich posterity. Likewise, good ones are soon forgotten. In his introduction, Bennett, referring to Philip Larkin's "This Be the Verse," which is reprinted in *Poetry in Motion* (*PM* 89), looks at both sides of the problem: the Parents of Art "never get it right. They bring up a child badly and he turns out a writer, posterity never forgives them—though without that unfortunate upbringing the writer might never have written a word. They bring up a child well and he never *does* write a word. Do it right and posterity never hears about the parents; do it wrong and posterity never hears about anything else" (*Kafka* xiii). No gentle, loving dad who starved his son's imagination with sweet nurture, the truculent Hermann galvanized that imagination and made it resonate. "I'm a bad father, so I'm in the text," Hermann says late in the play (*Kafka* 61).

He can be believed. This father figure plumes himself on authority, which, like Dad in *Enjoy,* he describes in sexual terms: "I had fifteen men under me," he says of the shop he owned (*Kafka* 38). This "emperor in the armchair" (*Kafka* xii) also had the knack of reducing his author-son to the level of a hapless juvenile. When Linda tells Franz, "You're a grown man," he replies immediately, "Not with my father around I'm not" (*Kafka* 40). Hermann stifles his son by design, his Laius complex stemming from his anger. He believes that Franz predeceased him out of spite, and now, in the afterlife, Hermann wants his name redeemed. He claims that Franz's image as "nice people" comes at his father's expense: "Thanks to me. Thanks to me being the shit" (*Kafka* 47). So determined is his pursuit of redemption that, besides resenting Brod's centricity in the Kafka legend, Hermann charges his son, the author of *The Trial* (1925), with bearing false witness (*Kafka* 51). The mock trial that ensues shows the extremes to which Hermann will go to redeem himself. He ridicules Franz, hugs and kisses him, and calls him both a "teetering column of urine" (*Kafka* 47) and a "two-faced pisspot" (*Kafka* 48), all because Franz is the only Kafka posterity remembers. But then Franz always hated his name and did his best to suppress it. His failure undergirds one of the wildest ironies in literary history, the first initial of his last name having become one of the most famous in modern letters.

Hermann's chief weapon against his son—implied by the diminishing insults he uses—declares itself in the play's title. Whereas Hermann's penis was large, Franz's was small, and he was self-conscious about it. Hermann's associating his son with urine (*Kafka* 47, 48), a waste product, rather than with life-

giving sperm also makes Franz wince, partly because the association hits home. Franz had no children. Though he patronized
whores, he conducted his serious love affairs by mail. And it is
urine that brings him to life in the play. He has returned to earth
as a tortoise, an apt enough guise for one who often likened
himself to animals in his writing. But even as a tortoise, he cannot escape his past. Losing bladder control while passing Sydney
and Linda's suburban home, Brod, enacting a metaphor that extends into what follows, accidentally pisses on the tortoise.

Kafka's ability to rise above stench and waste is only a passing concern. It soon becomes clear that he has already transcended
himself, his immortality having wafted him above earthly categories. He has also moved out of the range of Hermann's malice. After threatening to disclose Franz's most desperate secret,
Hermann does finally speak out, but to no avail. A University of
North Carolina Press book written by two psychology profes-
sors had already described Kafka as underendowed; the smallness of his penis has been common knowledge for some time,
and nobody cares. Kafka's anxiety has been groundless. He can
enter heaven without misgivings. Naturally, his eternal home is
run by Hermann, God the Father. "We're here for ever, you and
me," says Hermann after greeting his son in heaven (*Kafka* 67).
And he is right. If the great writer Dostoyevsky, who is mentioned in the play (*Kafka* 38), saw all fathers as images of God,
Franz Kafka need not chide himself for deifying Hermann. Means
cannot be sundered from ends. Hermann's elevation chimes with
the process that has made Franz a modern classic.

Another figure with a claim on Kafka is Sydney, "a mild
middle-aged" (*Kafka* 10) English insurance man. Kafka worked

in insurance, too, a coincidence that inspired Sydney to write an essay about him for a professional journal. But the two men share more besides working at the same job. Both dislike their names, and both have been tuberculosis patients. In fact, Linda helped nurse Sydney back to health, just as she later defends Kafka during his mock trial. Their links to Linda have thus helped both men. And though Kafka never usurps Sydney's husbandly office, he *is* found by Sydney in Linda's arms after an innocent mishap. It is suitable, moreover, that Sydney is accompanied by Brod when he finds the two together. Brod has noticed Sydney's dismissiveness toward Linda, and now that his literary hero, Kafka, has materialized, Sydney scarcely notices Linda at all. Kafka's effect on Sydney continues to show the corrosiveness of artistic endeavor. Based on what he has learned by entertaining Kafka in his home, Sydney hopes to expand the little article he was writing into a book that will change the direction of Kafka studies.

Little help will come from Sydney's aging father, who, in his incontinence and imminent transfer to a senior citizens' home, evokes both Joyce Chilvers's mother in *A Private Function* and the Cravens in *Enjoy*. The character known only as Father represents the negative pole of the powerful father archetype. He appears on stage in his weakness, a state that exerts a curious force. He supplies the Zimmer frame, or walker, that is used in act 2 to symbolize the dock in which Kafka stands trial. Father's association with the frame rivets Kafka; to walk away would constitute an act of paternal defiance beyond Kafka's powers. Thus Father is more than a victim. Or if he is a victim, he is a human one, like Kafka. Father's suffering matters. His words,

"Somebody's been telling lies about me. They've come to take me away" (*Kafka* 32), spoken in act 1, repeat nearly verbatim the first sentence of *The Trial,* which Brod quotes instructively about a minute before Father voices his anxiety. Perhaps Joseph K, the book's narrator, and Kafka, Joseph's creator, are consubstantial with Father and, by extension, with all fathers, an idea that gains strength from the venue of the play's last scene, heaven.

The remaining householder whose routine is broken by the incursion of the Kafka circle is Linda. She, too, partakes of the unity invoked by the play's last scene. Like Kafka, she is a loner. The three other men in the play all find her more interesting than does Sydney, who both misunderstands and devalues her. What Sydney has overlooked or forgotten about in Linda is her inner radiance; her instincts are sound and her heart is right. Because, unlike Sydney, Hermann, and Brod, she makes no claims on Kafka, she moves closer to him than they do. She likes him for himself, not for what she can get out of him. He welcomes her disclosure that she has read none of his work.

This former nurse, a true healer, knows how to boost a person's spirits. She and Kafka laugh together. During an exchange of a drinking glass, she contrives to have their fingers touch, a development that might have led to a kiss had they not been interrupted. But her commitment to him does not need to be ratified by kissing. When Sydney advises Kafka to talk to Hermann, she scotches the idea; interacting with Hermann can only wound Kafka. She defends him against Hermann's attacks. She comforts him by explaining that even though he's the source of the word *Kafkaesque,* he will probably never hear it said because he is known by only a tiny minority of people. And even though she tries to force food on him, she satisfies one of his deeper cravings—for privacy and anonymity. She defends him in court because she wants to shield him, mostly from her husband, who wants to gain fame at his expense.

The self-deprecating Kafka takes the brunt of such attacks just as he consents to his mock trial, which only his low self-esteem keeps him from walking away. Perhaps he cannot help himself. All his life, this walking contradiction sought both fame and obscurity. The play's first scene, which takes place in 1919 or 1920, shows him, a dying husk, telling Brod to destroy everything he, Kafka, ever wrote. Catching his drift, Brod promises to burn his friend's work: "it's burn, baby, burn," he says with relish (*Kafka* 7). His words bring out Kafka's self-division, as Brod knew they would. Kafka shrinks from the obscurity he craves. The prospect of fame even beguiles him. The celebrity enjoyed by his contemporary Marcel Proust rankles, and looking into the future, Kafka wants to share the honor of having the Nazis burn his books alongside those of Proust, Brecht, and Joyce. To be destroyed in such fine company would enshrine, rather than nullify, Kafka's work. Part of him would welcome this enshrinement, though he would never admit it. At the start of act 2, he glances furtively at one of his books, as if ashamed to let on, even to himself, that it interests him.

This ambiguity extends past his work. Early in act 1, scene 1, Kafka jokes about his impending death, reaffirming to Brod his promise to die soon (*Kafka* 5). Yet he can also be very stubborn. Early in act 2, he rejects, within a thirty-second time span, overtures from Linda, Brod, and Hermann (*Kafka* 44). But what if he *is* contrary? Contrariness is but one of his many failings. In fact, Sydney had built his essay-in-progress around his flaws. Having wrongly believed Kafka a saint, Sydney now realizes, "He has faults like everybody else" (*Kafka* 45). Perhaps Sydney will conclude that these faults elevate Kafka rather than degrade him. To write his fresh, revolutionary fiction, he had to overcome terrible psychic burdens. In the spirit of Linda Loman's famous "Attention must be paid" speech in Arthur Miller's *Death of a Salesman* (1949), Linda in *Kafka's Dick* proclaims Kafka's importance. Even if his exertions did recoil upon each other and proved self-canceling, they matter because they came from him; his very existence gives them meaning: "although you despair," she tells him, "you believe your despair is important. You think you're insignificant but your insignificance is not insignificant" (*Kafka* 57).

He cannot be insignificant, and, by extension, neither can Brod or Hermann, since they are so bound up with him. Otherwise, Hermann would not have reappeared in heaven as God, and Brod would not have come back to earth without his hunchback. Kafka's translation is different. A born loser, he has swathed himself in gloom and sorrow. When Linda asks if he is disappointed in her, he answers, "No. I always expect to be disappointed. If I'm not disappointed, then I'm disappointed" (*Kafka* 57). But there is more to say. Kafka has fulfilled the conditions for redemption by denying them. After entering heaven at the end, he claims to be in the wrong place. But "the celestial construct" (*Kafka* 65), or divine logic, governing requirements for admission into heaven disproves his claim. By insisting that he does not deserve a place in heaven, he has confirmed his worthiness to God. His belief in his unfitness proves him fit.

It is the smug and the prideful who do not belong in heaven. Kafka's final words show that he can stand together with the saints just the way he is. Linda was right about his importance; he need not reform. "I'll tell you something. Heaven is going to be hell" (*Kafka* 67), he says of his celestial future, mustering the same backhandedness that probably tainted all the blessings that ever came his way. Everything is where it should be. The hellishness of heaven certifies its heavenly radiance. And Kafka has reverted to his usual practice of inverting values and then coming out on top. The first and last speeches of the play belong to him; his words swathe the action. He has also made it to heaven, a passage foreshadowed by his earlier appearance as a tortoise, symbol of immortality.

The tortoise symbolism puts a comic spin on the idea, one more American (and Russian) than British, that tragedy holds the seeds of saving grace. Kafka always identified with animals in his fiction, sometimes lowly ones like mice or beetles. By shrinking, he elevated himself into the first rank of European writers; burrowing into obscure crannies and cubbyholes cleared him a path to posterity. Perhaps in his tortoise aspect, he was looking for a hiding place when Brod emptied his bladder on him. Maybe Brod began pissing on Kafka by publishing his manuscripts, writing his biography, and making a cottage industry of lecturing on his old friend. But a little piss cannot faze the ex-nurse Linda. She cleans the tortoise under a tap and then kisses it. Her kiss brings it to human life in a variation of the frog-and-prince paradigm that works at several dramatic levels. First, the incident evokes the category of the beast fable, of which Kafka wrote many. Next, being peed on led him to Linda, whom he

would not have met otherwise. Being a victim has helped him,
just as his practice of writing about unfortunates like the Hunger
Artist and Gregor Samsa of *The Metamorphosis* (1915) would
win him international fame. What falls also rises.

A final example of Kafka's ability to inflict worse harm on
himself than Hermann or Brod could ever cause comes in the
play's title. Even before Kafka appears in the play, Sydney and
Linda discussed the University of North Carolina book, *Dreams,
Life, and Literature,* particularly the part where the authors, Hall
and Lind, argue convincingly that Kafka was underendowed. As
was mentioned earlier, being underendowed is Kafka's deepest
shame and darkest secret. Every one of Hermann's allusions to
it makes him cringe. He could have spared himself these ago-
nies. Throughout the play, Hermann tortures his son by threatening to divulge something the world already knew and did not
set much store by. As Linda tells the son in her decent, sensible
way, "your private parts have been public property" (*Kafka* 61).

Naturally, she speaks out because Hermann, malevolent as
ever, had just shamed him by going public with his worst fear.
Hermann's words have changed nothing. Despite the smallness
of his penis, Kafka remains an artist hero, while the well-hung
Hermann will always be a puny villain. "Same old Hermann,"
says Brod (*Kafka* 61). And same old Kafka. The disclosure he
has been dreading relieves him, taking him beyond Hermann's
malice. Yet he feels defeated; Hermann has bested him again.
Unsoothed by Linda's comforting words, Kafka is still his father's
victim. But perhaps complaints are out of order. He is used to
this misery, defines himself by it, and uses it as the psychological building blocks of his vision.

KAFKA AND OTHER OFFICE DRONES

Other aspects of the script provide fun. For a work that portrays the suffering of one of the century's best-known sufferers, *Kafka's Dick* is full of laughs. There is Sydney's epigrammatic wit: "In England, facts . . . pass for culture. Gossip is the acceptable face of intellect" (*Kafka* 64). Sydney and the others also communicate their awareness that they are fictional characters. Brod says in act 2, "If I hadn't been Kafka's friend there would have been no play" (*Kafka* 62). The Bennett of *Kafka's Dick* may have been thinking of Roland Barthes's decree in *The Rustle of Language* (1986) that the author has died and of Jacques Derrida's pronouncement in "Signature, Event, Context" (1977) that no literary work has a context. The notion of the text as a unit of meaning or of sound has yielded to that of the text as romper room. Sydney, who has scholarly ambitions, says soon after showing his face, "One of the functions of literary criticism is to point out unexpected connections" (*Kafka* 13). At times, *Kafka's Dick* invites connections, but only to renounce them. The characters' occasional practice of addressing the audience (e.g., *Kafka* 15, 41) blurs the urgency of the proceedings and brightens the tone, Kafka's onstage presence generating a gloom that might otherwise oppress.

Oppressive Kafka can be. The other characters refer to Gregor Samsa of *Metamorphosis* as a cockroach (e.g., *Kafka* 8, 12) despite Kafka's ongoing insistence that Gregor became a beetle. (Even Kafka's biggest supporter, Linda, asks when he first got "the writing bug" [*Kafka* 35].) Writers cannot control posterity's response to their work, because readers have always bent literary texts to whatever intellectual or artistic fad is in vogue. Perhaps the many ironies springing from Kafka's prac-

tice of finding happiness or at least peace in sorrow makes meaning tricky and elusive. When Sydney draws his living room curtains and places his father's walker around Kafka to invoke a
courtroom, he sounds a note of persecution, perhaps even of
sadism. Death would suit Kafka better than this badgering. Perhaps Linda, who never read a word of Kafka, has the best idea:
"Most people have never heard of either of you," she says after
Kafka voices some words of envy about Proust's achievements
(*Kafka* 42).

II

The 1986 BBC-TV2 teleplay *The Insurance Man* is a brilliant, brooding, hard-edged rendering of the damage inflicted
on the soul by the modern industrial state. Like its companion
piece, *Kafka's Dick, The Insurance Man* ends with a tailpiece,
or coda, that leaps ahead in time from its main action. It also
opens with a short sequence decades in time away from the pri-
mary action. But *The Insurance Man* includes a time twist.
Whereas *Kafka's Dick* opens in 1919 or 1920 before jumping
ahead to the 1980s, *The Insurance Man,* opening in 1945, seats
most of its plot thirty-five years earlier. The work's main setting
is Prague's Workers Accident Insurance Institute, "where Kafka,"
Bennett says, "was a conscientious and well-thought-of executive" (*Kafka* 71). One of Kafka's clients in the teleplay is a twenty-
six-year-old dye worker named Franz. As his name suggests,
Franz is a working-class foil of sorts to Kafka. Both men are
about the same age, and both are popular with women. They
also work in the same asbestos factory, where they contract the

lung disorders that help kill them. But Franz has a tender, loving relationship with his peasant father (Hermann neither appears nor is mentioned in the play), and, a fine gymnast, he is also healthier than his tubercular alter ego.

Franz has reached a crossroad. He has just become engaged to a young woman, Christina, a cut or so above him socially. But he is forced to question the security of their engagement. A progressive skin disorder jeopardizes his future with Christina. The patch he finds on his hand soon develops into a rash, followed by some scaling. Soon he is in the same bind that squeezes the prototypical Kafka hero; he has been given a task that cannot be completed but also must be completed. The dye with which Franz has been working has both burned and infected his skin. But rather than treating him, his chiefs at the dye works fire him. When he goes to the insurance institute, he is foiled again when his claim for compensation is rejected. Technically, he is told, his rash was no accident. He could not avoid being splashed by the dye with which he was working—being splashed is an everyday reality of his job. On the other hand, he did blister his skin at the dye bath. Had he been working elsewhere in the plant, his skin would still be smooth and clear.

As in *Kafka's Dick,* guilt connects the characters of *The Insurance Man.* Bennett has a kindly, sympathetic insurance executive tell a claimant, "Just because you're the injured party, it doesn't mean you are not the guilty party" (*Kafka* 95). Guilt also gnaws at Franz (as might be expected in Kafka's alter ego). To assuage this guilt, Franz waives financial compensation. He appears naked before an auditorium full of doctors and medical students because he wants them to give a name to his skin problem. The problem must be named before it can be diagnosed and treated. Bennett's introduction uses legalistic language to describe Franz's plight: "He wants his offence identified but no one will give it a name; this is his complaint. Until his offence is named he cannot find a tribunal to acquit him of it" (*Kafka* xvi). Withholding a name from something counts as a denial of its existence in Bennett. The unnamed datum can be shrugged off and forgotten. Like many of Bennett's (and some of Kafka's) people, Franz has persisted in his search for his rightful place. The gamble he takes by offending the tribunal of doctors and medical students recalls Pascal's bet: though the odds are long, the potential prize is huge, making the placing of the bet eminently worthwhile. Franz does not get a name for his disease. But he does get a reprieve, which, in typical Kafka fashion, hits him harder than his original complaint.

"Kafka's good turn sealed Franz's death warrant," says Bennett in the diary he kept while the teleplay was in production (*Kafka* 72). The world is so dreadful that the helping hand of a deliverer or savior can inflict death. Such a sour irony befits someone whose family, Kafka believed, ruined his chance for happiness. The members of Kafka's home need not appear in person for their baleful influence to be felt. A satellite member can deliver the blow. On and off between 1911 and 1917, Kafka had helped run his brother-in-law's asbestos factory. Bennett's Kafka feels sorry when Franz leaves the institute with empty hands and a heavy heart. Not that Kafka is surprised by his colleagues' dismissiveness; he has long since known of their tendency to marshal any excuse to rule against a claimant. Yet he soldiers on as well as he can. Like any other skilled bureaucrat,

KAFKA AND OTHER OFFICE DRONES

he sees that he must use tact and indirection to reach his goals. In a speech given at a party honoring his department head, Kafka hews to the party line, mocking the claimants and the allegedly feeble claims with which they worry the institute's capable, conscientious staffers every day. By deflecting the professional envy of these staffers, many of whom would like the prestige of speaking at the department head's party, Kafka is better able to provide the odd claimant some off-the-record help.

But the help may conceal a time bomb. Franz's year or two in the asbestos factory sufficed to plant the needlelike fibers in his lungs that would kill him thirty years later. On the credit side, the dermatitis he incurred at the dye factory might have driven him mad had Kafka not given him a new start. His mysterious rash might have even killed him (dye can make you die, runs Bennett's implied pun). Nor is the clearing of Franz's skin his only sign of renewal. He applies for a job at the asbestos factory with his fiancée at his side. The fiancée is Beatrice, the secretary who extended kindness to him at the dye works. Christine, the woman to whom he was engaged at the start of the play, broke with him after discovering his skin problem. No great loss to Franz: she would have never given him the support needed to endure two wars, let alone the travails of domesticity. Beatrice probably made him a happier home than he would have had with Christine. And he only met Beatrice because of his trouble at the dye works. Kafka's fatal intervention bought him more than time. Not that time should be derided; Franz is still alive at the close. Even though the image of a hanged man both begins and ends the teleplay, this grisly portent might bypass him. He thought he was a "goner" before World War I broke out (*Kafka* 86). This ex-gymnast could have the stamina to survive physically just as his alter ego, who predeceased him by some twenty years, has survived spiritually because of his outstanding imaginative breakthroughs.

The divisions in that alter ego run as deep in *The Insurance Man* as they did in *Kafka's Dick.* Kafka is an insurance officer and a father-ridden author in both plays. Even though his light side dominates in *The Insurance Man,* his noonday virtues—his kindness, his tact with colleagues, and his eagerness to help strangers—lead to the dark. Nor would the dark upshot of his actions surprise him. In *Kafka's Dick,* he called himself "a terrible human being" (*Kafka* 56). And he does act in *The Insurance Man* as if his benevolence stems from either an unspoken urge to quiet his nagging guilt or, more poignantly, a sympathy with what Cardinal Newman called "the terrible aboriginal calamity" governing the human estate. Whereas Kafka's colleagues mock the claimants who come to the institute, Kafka tries to help them, even going beyond his charter to relieve suffering. Using some fancy verbal capework with a disaffected colleague, he restores Franz to his caseload. And when Franz shows up in his office, he is polite, saying "Please" and offering his visitor a seat (*Kafka* 122).

Kafka's belief that justice "doesn't exist in the world" (*Kafka* 122) has convinced him of the importance of bestowing kindness in its place. His job has sharpened his appreciation of kindness. Not only do his coworkers find ways to bilk the claimants out of their just compensation, but the claimants also downgrade each other's claims, suspecting that they can help their own chances by disparaging those of their rivals. This war of all against all gains momentum from the sad truth that most of the claims brought to the institute are disallowed.

Kafka (who is played stunningly by Daniel Day Lewis) defines the term *accident* more imaginatively than do the claimants, as well he might. Having been emotionally scarred at home (*Kafka* xiv), he identifies with them. If he cannot dispense justice to them, he can at least offer them some peace or, as in Franz's case, time. The bureaucracy has not shackled him. As he showed in *The Trial,* the civil servant Kafka saw himself as a member of a society so inscrutable that it could summon up a nonexistent law to kill an innocent person for having performed an unknown crime. Perhaps that crime is so bound up with being human that it need not be committed to warrant punishment. Kafka comes close to saying in *The Insurance Man* that people deserve compensation for being alive. Evil and death are everywhere. Franz not only infected himself by breathing in the wrong place—the asbestos works. He got sick, rather, by simply breathing.

A black comedy about corporate bad faith, *The Insurance Man* conjures up the landscape of Kafka's mind. It also describes the office politics prevailing at the institution where Franz and Kafka meet. Included in the byplay between the employees are the guarded attempts at friendship among people of different social and official rank. When these employees are not jockeying to advance themselves within the system, they are protecting their turf. Avoiding controversy abets self-protection. Thus they try to disclaim responsibility for pronouncing on a claimant's degree of disability. Some of the claims facing them add up to huge sums, and none of them wants to be caught wasting the firm's money. Money can humbug the staffers in different forms.

They are no more enamored of contributing to a going-away present for their boss than they are of compensating a claimant. But contribute they do, with a show of cheer lest they be caught committing a political gaffe.

Everybody feels the strain induced by answering to a bizarre morality, a condition captured by the illogic and intricacy (*Kafka* 94) governing the firm's physical layout. Bennett discusses this morality in his introduction: "It must have been a strange place, the Workers Accident Insurance Institute. . . . It was a world where to be deprived was to be endowed, to be disfigured was to be marked out for reward and to trip was to jump every hurdle" (*Kafka* xv). Theological issues have again pushed to the fore. A context in which loss means gain and where wretchedness reaps rewards evokes the passage in the Book of Matthew (19:30) ordaining that the last go first. But the institute's prevailing morality slights the resemblance. Kafka and Pohlmann probably have other colleagues who can match them in kindness and compassion. But they would be in the minority. Handsome young Culick fondles a pretty stenographer in the presence of a claimant who recently lost an ear in an industrial accident. Another colleague, Gutling, takes out his resentment over his low ranking in the firm by herding some clients together and then shouting them out of the office. Neither will Gutling have to worry about answering for his cruelty to his chiefs.

A mood conducive to cruelty was established at the beginning of the play. Guns and bombs were heard going off in the outskirts of 1945 Prague, and a corpse allegedly belonging to an enemy of the occupying Soviets came into view hanging from a lamppost. This same corpse reappears in the play's final scene

and stays on-screen during the rolling of the credits, Franz having just left the office of the doctor who pronounced his death
sentence. The cordite-reeking Prague into which Franz walks is
but one ugly portent Bennett uses to reinforce the work's pessi-
mism. Waiting to be interviewed by caseworkers at the institute
are claimants with a bandaged neck, a missing leg, and deep
facial scars. The disappointment awaiting most of them is pre-
figured by the sharp, snapping machinery that comes into view
several times during the action, a circular saw and an elevator,
the gates of which are photographed to look like scissors or a
guillotine. Such fresh, convincing details help re-create the convoluted inner energy of Prague in the last days of the Hapsburg
Empire. This energy bounces crazily between Franz and Kafka.
Written with elegance and economy, *The Insurance Man* describes with Kafkaesque flair the psychological and spiritual burdens of surviving in a bureaucracy whose own survival depends
on acts of calculated cruelty and absurdity.

III

One Fine Day is one of six plays by Bennett filmed for
release on London Weekend Television in 1978–79. Unfolding
in a board room, a secretarial pool, an elevator, and a men's
room, it shows staffers of different kinds interacting both per-
sonally and vocationally. One canvasses the office collecting for
charity. Another voices her fear of losing her job to a computer.
The chairman of the London real estate firm in whose offices
the February 1979 telescript unfolds is called Welby. Always
speaking with the poise and breeding of the English public school

man, Welby has in hand the social skills that have won him success. As befits any good salesperson, he maintains a cheerful
front that sorts well with the confidence often needed to crush
sales resistance. Nothing seems to ruffle this jovial, outgoing
man. Yet, as the boss of a large firm responsible for millions of
pounds of real estate property, he must be calculating. Worried
that he may have offended George Phillips, the play's main figure, he asks about Phillips's family, referring to his wife by name.
Welby wants to learn as much as he can about his workers not
because he likes them but because he wants to maximize their
efficiency. And, as his words to a junior colleague show, making
money overrides all of his other considerations: "Selling. Business. That's what matters. What are toes for but to be trod on?"[2]
Velvet-gloved opportunism like this keeps his workers as nervous as any functionary in Kafka.

At the play's outset, Welby is conducting a meeting. Each
of the "dozen or so" (*WD* 115) sales executives he presides over
wants to advance himself. Yet each scrupulously avoids giving
the impression of overstepping limits in the name of self-
advancement. Above all, no one in the room wants to be caught
advancing himself at a colleague's expense. Thus a spirit of forced
egalitarianism and informality pervades the meeting, squash
partners exchanging smiles and addressing each other by their
first names. Yet all know this cozy collective persona to be a
ruse. Welby can overrule the others at any time. He has made it
clear that his firm exists to sell or rent buildings. The longer a
building stands unsold or unrented, the lower its market value.
More than reputation is at stake, though. Besides wanting to
dodge the notoriety of having invested badly, any real estate chief

has to worry about his exchequer. To unload ongoing tax pay-
ments and maintenance costs, he may lower his asking price for
an unsold building. The plot of *One Fine Day* begins with the
disclosure that George Phillips has failed to move Sunley House,
a large London office block, in the eighteen months he has been
in charge of its sale. His failure has made him fair game among
his ambitious colleagues, several of whom snipe at him during
the meeting. Phillips is a real estate agent in his late forties employed by the old established firm of Frobisher, Rendell, and
Ross. So elite is the firm, in fact, that none of the sales executives who appears on-screen has his name posted on the
company's logo. Presumably, its founders are long dead, a sign
of its longevity. Nor have underperformers like Phillips helped
it prosper in a competitive market. Phillips is feeling squeezed.
Seen both at home and at work, he displays himself in the round.
He is also the teleplay's most carefully developed character. Invoking the motif of the obsolete man, Bennett demonstrates that
this idler must get busy. Life in his family has been changing
quickly. His wife has a swarm of activities outside the home,
and his high-school-aged son has started to bring his girlfriends
home for both meals and sex (yet, in this play about usurpation,
Robin refuses to have sex in his parents' bed).

But the worries caused by Phillips's son and wife pale before those plaguing him at work. His job security is being threatened by a young favorite of Welby named Rycroft. Welby has
authorized Rycroft to take over the sale of Sunley House ("What
are toes for but to be trod on?"). The speed with which the le-
thargic Phillips takes action to drive this young poacher from
his turf shows that business colleagues can direct more suspi-

cion and wrath to each other than to functionaries of rival firms. Phillips's ruthlessness also reminds us that Bennett included *One Fine Day* in his 1985 collection *The Writer in Disguise*. Though no writer, Phillips knows the loneliness and disconnection afflicting writers during their long sessions at the desk. His solitary bent has given him the single-mindedness of the artist. Operating as covertly as that archetypal Irish writer, James Joyce's Stephen Dedalus, the Irish Phillips defrauds and deceives his colleagues to the point of putting them at risk.

He knows that both his low energy level and his lackadaisical tilt of mind bar him from using the same sales tactics as his colleagues. One is surprised that this furtive, antisocial man has survived in real estate, a clubbable line of work that usually attracts the warmhearted and the outgoing. He turns down invitations to lunch and drinks (*WD* 141, 154). Rather than articulate answers to questions, even from Welby, the boss, Phillips shakes or nods his head. When voiced, his answers are clipped and evasive. He has also impugned his credibility in the office. Besides acting bored and surly with his colleagues, he leaves work early (*WD* 122) and gives an impression of inefficiency. At the last minute, he is willing to call off an appointment to see some prospective buyers of Sunley. He seems in no hurry to sell the place referred to in the trade as White Elephant House (*WD* 132). Rather than looking for customers, he is content to wait for the right ones to come forward on their own, something he is sure will happen when the economy improves. Yet, as Welby points out at the board room meeting, the economy has already picked up, and no prospective buyer has come forth (*WD* 117). The twenty-five-year-old Rycroft is not taking much of a chance by asking to be put in charge of selling Sunley House, even though he sells residential rather than commercial properties.

Rycroft is only slightly more likeable than Phillips. A career that consists of showing suburban homes to "dismal little couples" (*WD* 134) is not what he wants. He would prefer working in the Persian Gulf, where his efforts could net him a giant-sized helping of money and sex (*WD* 131). This cub throws himself into the pursuit of his goals. Yes, these goals lack uplift, but he may outgrow them. And besides, his drive to get ahead will swell the earnings of any firm he works for. His ambition may not comfort his coworkers, though. Soon after learning that the sale of Sunley House has been turned over to Rycroft, Phillips sets out to sabotage the sale and with it Rycroft's image as a wunderkind. Phillips finagles his way into the building and spends the night on its rough, debris-strewn top floor. Then his physical courage helps him convert a career-ending disgrace into gain. Having climbed the stairs to the roof of Sunley to foil a security check, he hears the door leading back into the building being locked. He throws a brick attached to a rope through a top-floor window of the nine-story building. Overcoming his fear of heights, he slithers down the rope and climbs through the broken window. Then he acts with a farsightedness that would have made him his firm's top salesman had he implemented it on a daily basis.

The breaking of the window has already smudged Rycroft's shiny image since it happened on his watch. It does far more damage, though, wrecking his chances to sell Sunley to the American firm that has sent its agents to inspect the building. First, the incident makes the agents worry that Sunley stands in "a violent neighborhood," which would endanger the people passing in and out of it (*WD* 148). The Bible, the bedroll, and the cassette player that Phillips left behind worry the agents still more, making the building look as if it has been occupied by a squatter; security is poor at Sunley House. Rycroft must now take steps to keep Sunley from looking like a bad risk. Puzzled but determined, he sleeps on the building's top floor to fend off any other incursions, consoling himself with the gear that Phillips had left behind, as Phillips knew he would. Thus Phillips, looking to maximize his chances against Rycroft, makes an early-morning appointment for some Japanese to inspect the building. He wants Rycroft to be found sleeping on the unfinished top floor.

Everything proceeds on cue for Phillips. An unshaven Rycroft is discovered sleeping on Phillips's bedroll. "That's always a bad sign," says Welby of the Bible near Rycroft (*WD* 154). Perhaps unreliable, impulsive Rycroft does not belong in a solid "old-fashioned" firm like Frobisher, Rendell, and Ross, after all; "For his own sake," Welby fires him. (*WD* 154). Phillips has won the day. He has gotten rid of the much younger colleague Welby had been grooming to take his place, and he sells Sunley House, probably earning a fat commission in the process. His parting words to his boss convey a self-confidence that abuts on rudeness. Invited for a drink to celebrate the sale of Sunley, Phillips says simply, "I won't" (*WD* 154). His earlier belief that the sale of the building depended on twinning the right client to the right economic climate has been vindicated. Welby should never have doubted his judgment. Phillips would not think of celebrating with his boss and doesn't even thank him for the invitation.

This arrogance carries into the final scene, where Phillips refuses to let Robin's girlfriend spend the night. This development is disturbing. He seems to be making a pastime of thwarting younger males. The artist in Schopenhauer, Freud, and Mann is a ruthless outsider who turns from the crowd for the sake of self-creation. Phillips is last seen alone. His wife has gone upstairs, and Robin has taken June home. But even in the company of the family Phillips was alone, listening to music through a pair of headphones, a practice that stopped the others in the room from sharing his joy.

It is material that he is listening to music rather than playing or composing it. This loner, a parody of the artist, brings nothing of any consequence into the world. Unlike Joyce's Stephen Dedalus, another Irish outsider-rebel too proud to wear a mask, Phillips harbors no wish to revolutionize prose fiction or any other art form. He just wants to save his job, on which, instructively, he underperforms. But the wit and ingenuity he displays shoring up his place in the firm's hierarchy cause a great deal of damage. Often inclined to complex actions that end in a restoration of the status quo, Bennett portrays in *One Fine Day* the unraveling of the system that prevailed at the play's outset. In Rycroft, the firm has lost an employee far more valuable than Phillips. Phillips has also put to risk the career of Peggy Morpeth, the clerk in charge of issuing keys to sales properties, making her look careless and incompetent by filching the key to Sunley House behind her back. No doubt, Bennett intended Frobisher as a metaphor for the real estate trade. The action of *One Fine Day* makes one wonder not how the system turns a profit but rather how it survives.

This question invokes others. Why are the plumbing and electricity of the buildings we occupy still intact? And why haven't all of London's real-estate firms shut down? An answer to these questions lies two continents away, in the Far East. One of the musical selections Phillips listens to on his headphones is Puccini's *Madame Butterfly* (*WD* 126), a work that presents Asians as passive and submissive. Yet it is Asian industry and grit that save Phillips's job. Japanese business was pushing aggressively into the West in the late 1970s, particularly in the fields of real estate, automotives, and electronics. The Japanese buyers of Sunley House wanted a London power base and overlooked certain disincentives to gain one. Despite what Welby and Phillips might think, they have noted everything in Sunley during their reconnoiter. And they know enough about architecture to assess their chances accurately. Nor are their powers of assessment unique. Tokyo's office blocks stand higher than those in London despite the threat of earthquakes. Perhaps the Japanese buyers of Sunley spotted some potential in the place that raised its value above Welby's asking price.

The job's importance may grow in unexpected ways for Phillips. His son will be spending more and more time away from home now that Phillips has stopped allowing Robin's dates to spend the night. Phillips's wife seems to have already moved her base of operations away from the home. For some time, she has been studying subjects like lampshade making, conversational Spanish, and bookbinding. And why not? With his headphones clapped to his ears, Phillips provides her little companionship. She must feel blocked. She rarely completes the courses she takes, and a grapevine she planted has just died. And now she is faced with an emergency. This woman who is

associated with aborted projects has to care for her sick father in
Colchester. Her absence does free Phillips to prowl around
Sunley. But it is more than a plotting device. Twice, Phillips
sees the same couple kissing near Sunley (*WD* 135, 143). He
cannot escape the naked upsurge of the instincts. Sexual regret
haunts this man who lets his wife ascend the stairs to their bedroom by herself at play's end. Although he was shamming, he
did suggest to Welby that Rycroft may have been using Sunley
as a love nest (*WD* 154). He may have felt that his wife was
taking evening courses as a sex substitute. Perhaps he also doubts
that she spent her whole Colchester visit at her father's bedside.
He probably never phones her in Colchester because he does not
want to know.

The television camera lends weight to such issues. A character like Welby can be seen from Phillips's point of view while
discussing a subject vital to Phillips, like the transfer of the sale
of Sunley House to Rycroft. Producer/director Stephen Frears
practices a fine economy of means in *One Fine Day*. The skill
with which he coordinates the camera with Bennett's script helps
give a lively, realistic portrayal of office routine along with revealing glimpses of the main figure's mind. Frears's effects also
evoke the embarrassing moral and aesthetic gulf between British and American television drama in the late 1970s, a gulf that
the passage of years has preserved, if not widened.

IV

Shown on BBC–TV2 in late 1982, *Rolling Home* bears many
of the trademarks of its author. The play's title invokes the motif, common in Bennett, of life's irrevocable forward flow. Life

goes on in *Rolling Home* in a hospital for the elderly in which some of the patients ride in wheelchairs to the Assembly Hall for games and socializing. A familiar synapse has occurred. The North-of-England location of the hospital turns Bennett's creative energies to the family. As in *Enjoy,* the family unit Bennett explores in *Rolling Home* has been corroding, headed, as it is, by an aged, infirm patriarch named Wilfred who beat his wife and may have also molested at least one of his children. That child, a grown daughter named Val, has not taken to the streets like Linda Craven. But she does mention in passing fashion design centers like Paris and Milan, and, like Linda, she limps onto the set because her expensive new shoe has broken. Val has no cross-dressing brother, though. Instead, Bennett plays off this career girl of dubious morality against a conventional stay-at-home sister, Molly, who has a family of her own and resents the younger, more stylish Val for supposedly neglecting their father. Mirroring this rivalry of sisters is one involving two coworkers, both men. But the nurses Vic and Donald, who like and respect each other, would do nothing to sabotage each other's careers, even though they are competing for the same upgrade in rank.

The hospital where the men work would strain anybody's loyalty. Its black head nurse, Matron, and an Asian doctor—the highest-ranking members of the hospital staff who appear on-screen—emit a multicultural ambience evocative of the 1980s. Also redolent of Mrs. Thatcher's England is the impression the hospital gives of being both underfunded and understaffed. Vic and Donald look as if they have been run off their feet, dressing wounds, making sure the patients have paid their toilet calls, changing the incontinent, and, not least of all, chasing down patients who have slipped out of the building; since the patients have not been classified as dangerous, they can move about freely, which means that at least one of them has to be recaptured seventeen times in a day (*OA* 71).

Vic could work full time running his randy-mouthed patient, Mr. Riscoe, to earth. Yet Vic has the professionalism to keep up with his other chores as well. He spends less time on-screen than Donald because Donald has been assigned to look after Mr. Wyman, Val and Molly's father and thus the fulcrum of the play's major tensions. What Vic shows of himself, though, is engaging. Now it is clear that Matron, whose recommendation for the upgrading in rank carries weight, despises both Vic and Donald. On the other hand, her knowing that Vic is gay will probably swing her support to Donald. Besides, Donald has made it known that he needs the money that goes with the promotion to buy a home for himself and his bride-to-be. Vic is thus the underdog in the competition. What may hurt his chances still more is his mockery of Pam, the "jolly therapist in her thirties" (*OA* 64) who leads the songs and games during the patients' social hour in the Assembly Hall. Mr. Riscoe keeps disrupting the word games by tossing in scatological terms, a practice Vic encourages, to Pam's dismay. Were Matron to learn of Vic's japing, she would be even more inclined to vote against him for promotion than she already is.

Bennett keeps the Vic-Donald subplot in view. Fascinated by the dynamics of office politics, he builds an emotional counterpoint around the impending promotion. Vic has already shown us, through a dedication leavened by a sense of fun, that he deserves the upgrade. Yet Donald is also deserving. Patient, affectionate, and gentle, he always tries to comfort his charges. He calls Wilfred Wyman "Joey" because Wyman likes the name (*OA* 57). And Wyman calls *him* by name (*OA* 61), a grace he withholds from his daughters. Grateful for Donald's friendly attention, Wyman even calls Donald his "pal" (*OA* 68). But perforce some of Donald's attention goes to his fiancée. He and Jenny break hospital rules by spending time together during his work shift. Even though he is working nights because he needs the extra cash, he has less freedom than he had thought. Inviting Jenny to the hospital was a foolish risk. Caught in flagrante with her by the Matron, he forfeits the promotion he needed to scrape together the funds for a down payment on a home.

The patient he spends most of his time with, Wilfred, or Joey, Wyman, might know of these troubles. Were Wyman mentally fit, he would extend Donald sympathy. But senile and forgetful, he cannot keep track of the days of the week any more than he can remember his grandchildren's names. The condition of this elder worsens during the week or so it takes for the action to unfold. Loss of circulation has gangrened his leg, his incontinence has returned, and he keeps asking Donald what lies beyond the hospital wall. Though it is natural enough for an ex-bricklayer to wonder about walls, Wyman's wonderment transcends his old job. On the other side of the wall lies death, the lone mystery awaiting him. Late one night, he slides out of the ward for a look and then either slips or jumps into a nearby canal, where he drowns. In the spirit of Philip Larkin's poem "If This Be the Verse," which Bennett alluded to in *Kafka's Dick,* Wyman had asked Donald to tell an imaginary couple who live on the other side of the wall to remain childless. Wyman's daughters have resurrected his guilt. Nearing his end and prodded by memory, imagination, and a newly revived moral sense, he sees that Molly and Val, like all the other key players in his flawed, passionate life, have always known about his wife-beating. His daughters incarnate a guilt he will never shed. Why should he wish children on any other sinner who wants to reform? The very existence of children in the family reawakens the memory of sin.

Wyman gets more sympathy and support than he credits from his elder daughter, Molly. Molly had let him live with her and her family till his late-night rambles began upsetting the children. During her visitors'-day trips to the hospital, she voices concern for his progress, she spells out the activities of her children at the local sports center, and she has even given him a photo album filled with the children's pictures. But part of her exists outside the family orbit. Five minutes from the end of the play, it comes out that her birth name was Maureen. The Irish music and whimsy evoked by the name *Maureen* suggest a flair for fun and excitement she probably has not indulged for years. Imagination she has, this woman who has settled into the drabness of being Molly. Sitting near her father's hospital bed, she notes, "Your hands have gone nice, Dad. . . . Real lady's hands. Never think you were a bricklayer" (*OA* 53).

Even though she opted to become a homebody, it is still natural for her both to feel trapped and to resent her younger sister. Having chosen a career in fashion, Val drapes her trim figure in smart clothes, meets creative people, and has skipped most of the grind of elder care. But what else has she skipped? It is hard to know whether she is actuated by a drive to achieve or a drive to avoid. At times, she acts as if she is in hiding, mostly from herself. Her dream of Paris recalls Linda's Arabian fantasy in *Enjoy*. Val may be another besmirched daughter who wants to go abroad because she cannot find happiness at home. She seems to do well enough. As a buyer for an elegant gown shop, she has a better job than most career women her age. She has earned enough to buy a car and an answering machine. More tokens of occupational success may follow. Her boss, Mr. Stillman, thinks enough of her to send her to Manchester and Blackpool on assignment (*OA* 78). But her romantic self-image overrides these places. She claims that if she did not have to tend Dad, she would be working out of London. And from there, she would improve her chances of making it to her treasured Paris.

Should her thoughts be elsewhere? Molly berates her for neglecting their father. But neither sister has a preemptive hold on the truth. Molly, feeling dowdy and slow, seeks meaning through children who find her boring. Val enjoys more freedom, which she has used to attain a better wardrobe, a smarter figure, and more tasteful speech. Yet she lacks Molly's rootedness, and she has all but given up looking to set down roots. Childless herself, she resents hearing about her niece and nephews. Even though she would not want to trade places with Molly, Val feels unfulfilled, unreal, and perhaps even cheap. She grouses a good deal. But perhaps her complaints about the traffic en route to the hospital, about the hospital's administration, and about the shoddy care her father is ostensibly receiving say more about her than she intended. Having a little ballast in her life would make her less self-absorbed and less carping. Yet putting the ballast there calls for more courage and faith than she can afford. This brittle, easily rattled spinster is quick to blame others because, blameworthy herself, she wants to move out of the line of verbal fire.

Val is also upset that Molly has stowed their father in "a corporation place" (*OA* 59), a public health care facility, rather than a private one. Perhaps she is objecting to differences in the quality of service. More likely, she is recoiling from the stigma of having it known that her father is in Moortown, particularly by her boss, who may also be her lover. Her testiness, her quickness to find fault, and her escapist immersion in work all describe the careerist who either lacks good emotional support systems or who has emotional support systems she has to keep dark. Although she denies Molly's charge that she and Mr. Stillman are lovers, she has had plenty of time to frame her denial. She is also adept at deflecting verbal attack. Remembering a bruise on her mother's face, she has already accused her father of killing her. But if it did not stem from an old hurt, the accusation may have been merely an attempt to relieve pressure on herself.

There is no evidence to back the claim that Wyman raped Val. But her anger toward her father, her habit of avoiding her family, and her never having married all imply the distrust of intimacy that would haunt an abused child. Her alleged affair with Stillman invokes the same implication. Having a married lover would suit someone who wants excitement but knows that family living can break hearts. The possibility that Wyman abused

Val stays alive. Wyman does admit to having hit his wife (*OA* 79). On the subject of killing her, he says nothing. But Molly defends him anyway. Hearing Val's accusation, she says, "No. . . . It was Gilbert dying that killed mother" (*OA* 71). This lone mention of Gilbert in the teleplay suggests with more than Bennett's usual subtlety that Gilbert was the girls' gay brother; gay brothers figure in both *Enjoy* and *Marks* (1982). Each of these Bennett scripts, moreover, implies that the brother was abused by his father. Yet both brothers survive, albeit as half-lifers. Gilbert may have been less sturdy.

The strong sense of subtext in *Rolling Home* discourages moral judgments. But Val may have acted wisely by staying single. That she hobbles off stage carrying a broken shoe in her hand blunts some of her dignity, as it is meant to do. Bennett has a fine sense of incongruity, and he knows how to deploy it. Right after Wyman reaches into his psyche and voices his warning against having children, he wets himself; the little ordeal has crushed his reserves. The play's final scene, though, shows Bennett's instinct for rising to a climax in moments where climax works better than counterpoint or qualification. Vic and Donald are tending a patient. But Vic, carrying a clipboard and wearing the insignia of his higher rank, is obviously in charge. And authority is what he is supposed to project. The play ends with his asking Donald, "Could you see to this, nurse?" (*OA* 84). Thus the play's last word puts the seal on a completed action. This brilliant television play has many tensions, some of them overlapping. Thanks to Bennett's skill at orchestrating them, they form a neat package without forfeiting liveliness, warmth, and emotional complexity.

V

The Englishness of Bennett's people gains emphasis from the plays' North-of-England venues. Unlike American literary figures who feel free to move on and start over when their prospects sour (for example, Huck, Gatsby, and Bellow's Henderson), Bennett's people follow the English practice of taking what you have been given and settling for it. One character in *Green Forms* (1978) refuses to enroll in a computer course that would improve her prospects in the firm where she has been working: "I don't want prospects. Prospects is what I don't want."[3] Her foil replies to the suggestion that she join the employees' union by citing her husband: "Me and Cliff that's the only union I'm interested in" (*GF* 11). Doris and Doreen have narrowed it down; they are searching for ways to keep what they have. Perhaps they are wise. As a rule, North-of-Englanders in Bennett who see the territory ahead as a path to self-betterment are frauds, like Linda Craven of *Enjoy,* or malcontents, like Val Wyman of *Rolling Home.*

The habit of narrowing invokes both Kafka and the insecurity gripping the United Kingdom during the recession of the late 1970s. Insecurity is the norm of *Green Forms,* one of the two short television plays comprising Bennett's *Office Suite.* The coworkers Doris Rutter and Doreen Bidmead enjoy gossiping about the firm's badminton tournament or flirting with a man in a different department. But the economic woes of the day have also made them mindful of graver topics like layoffs, firings, and employee transfers. The women feel unsafe. They have lost track of the many policy changes framed by their chiefs. Computers requisitioned to speed the flow of work are already being phased out in favor of newer models. Closer to home, the green forms that refer to personnel decisions no longer go to the familiar Mrs. Henstridge but to the Newcastle office. As for Mrs. Henstridge, she has been sent to the firm's computer center in Garstang, and her daughter has gone to the Solomon Islands. A reference to Saudi Arabia (always a symbol of blasted hopes in Bennett) in a different context shows that changes in the world of business have disoriented the two women. Doris and Doreen have trouble siting themselves. They operate in the world of large, powerful multinationals, with its state-of-the-art technology, and also in the grotty little office which they report to every workday at 9:30 A.M.

The homey can vex them as much as the high-tech glitz. The requisitioning of a lampshade or a lightbulb takes more time and work than it should, the coworkers believe. And sometimes the requisitioned item is a wash-basin plug now that a personnel staffer has been stealing the plugs from the bathroom sink adjoining Doris and Doreen's office. Such little frustrations look like the work of a fiendish high-level bureaucrat out of Kafka. Perhaps they infer a Kafkaesque hierarchy whose continuance (as in "The Penal Colony") depends on the annihilation of its functionaries. The process seems well under way. Eroding the morale and thus the well-being of the workers is the firm's lack of guidelines and standards. A one-armed messenger embodies this disconnection. Not only was Frank Lomax's arm severed from his body in Britain's African Campaign against Rommel, but the union leader to whom Lomax reports has never even heard of either the campaign or the 1967 movie *Tobruk,* which depicted it. Appearing on the small screen are employees named Doris, Doreen, and Dorothy. On staff, as well, are a Diana, a Deirdre, and a Dorcas (*GF* 12). The corporate structure hammers down individuality. Since the great collective fear of the firm's employees is redundancy, the viewer worries about the competence these flattened selves will bring to a highly competitive job market after getting their pink slips.

Competence and capability are virtues far removed from the everyday operation of the Precepts and Invoices Department, the cluttered, run-down, and even grungy office where Doris and Doreen work. A lamp, a venetian blind, a broken door handle, and a window all need servicing. These "dilapidations" (*GF* 1) reflect both the laxity and the ineffectiveness of the office's occupants. What is more, the tatty office gives the impression of existing in a void. The women's supervisors have either forgotten about the place or do not care about it. At the outset, folders are stacked on chairs in the computerless room, and, rather than trying to organize them, Doris is reading a newspaper while Doreen gazes pointlessly at her desk. A further sense of wrongness comes across in an unoccupied third desk, a site that grows in importance as the one-acter moves ahead.

The possibility that the third desk will soon be occupied rattles Doris and Doreen, particularly if the occupant is to be one Dorothy Binns. Ms. Binns, whose name keeps cropping up, has worked at four different branch offices of the firm, all of which have since shut down. She may have been assigned to the Precepts and Invoices Department for the purpose of closing it. Though neglected by upper management, the department may have all along been under the eye of the CEO. But just before the end, Frank Lomax, the messenger, brings apparent relief. Perhaps the women can continue their regimen of reporting to work at a soft, convenient 9:30 A.M. after all. Lomax has no record of the impending arrival at the branch office of a Dorothy Binns. And his information turns out to be correct. But Ms. Binns, the specialist in downsizing, does not appear on Lomax's list of new-comers because she has already arrived.

Her back-lit appearance on screen at the end accounts for the teleplay's double-whammy finale. Ms. Binns's only line, "I am Work. I am Work" (*GF* 265), which closes the piece, would seem to justify her new office mates' worst fears. Accompany-ing her arrival on the set is an ominous black shadow. She has, moreover, renounced her name, flat and utilitarian sounding as it is, to identify herself with work. She belongs to a new breed of workaholic; whereas Bennett identifies Doris as *Miss* and Doreen as *Mrs.* in his list of characters, he designates the script's third speaking role as *Ms.* Ms. Binns will start applying pressure straightaway. Doris has pried her desk open and discovered, along with some freshly sharpened pencils, a nameplate and an apple, this last item suggesting banishment from paradise in Bennett's meandering comedy of menace. Ms. Binns arrived at the office long before Doris and Doreen and spent enough time there to put some things in her desk before locking it. And this is the desk that Doris has forced open.

How will she explain her petty vandalism? She and Doreen claim that they leave their desks unlocked because they trust each other. Of at least equal weight is the truth that they do little that is vital, confidential, or worth protecting from the eyes of others. Ms. Binns's presence in the office is justified; she has not sprung from the brow of a senior executive who operates with the inscrutability of a god or a senior bureaucrat out of Kafka. No self-starters, Doris and Doreen need to be brought up to speed. And if their messiness and inefficiency typify the branch office, as they well may (*GF* 25), then the drastic change Ms. Binns has been identified with is in order. The firm's survival could depend on reducing the number of its employees.

Also redolent of Kafka is the relationship of Lomax and his fellow messenger, Boswell. Though able-bodied, Boswell lets his one-armed colleague open the door to Doris and Doreen's office and unload the files from the trolley. Yet once inside the office, Lomax addresses his words to Boswell as if beholden to him. This odd behavior suggests the guilt displayed in *The Insurance Man* by the claimants, who cringe rather than demanding their rights from the institute's inspectors; people are more likely to truckle to their persecutors than to stand up to them, a motif enacted by Kafka with his father and also grazed in works like Kafka's *Castle* (1926).

A parody of Lomax's relationship with Boswell comes in the bond between Doris and Doreen. Both ties express what Bennett calls in his introduction to *Office Suite* a northern trait. "Social distinctions are subtle and minute" (*OS* 8) in England's industrial North, Bennett says of his ex-neighbors, a people, he adds, who have been taught to expect he worst. He shows, too, particularly in *Green Forms,* that in straitened circumstances the rare bounty takes on extra value because of its rarity. Coworkers threatened by unemployment will cling to their official status as to a life raft; they want to save their jobs. But, as Doris learns, one's official and social status can be skewed. Nor does one's job guarantee happiness and fulfillment. Like Val Wyman of *Rolling Home,* Doris worries excessively about small details and, because of her insecurity, frets disproportionately over minor setbacks.

This "unmarried lady in her forties" (*GF* 1) who lives with her mother also frets over aging. Perhaps Doreen has taken Doris's measure, saying that she would stow her mother in a nursing home in a heartbeat if a man looked twice at her (*GF* 21). If the ironically named Miss Rutter wants a rutting partner, she will have to act quickly. But age is not her only enemy. She will also have to check her bad temper and her passion to control. The frustrations stemming from work cause wear and tear on both women. And, though they direct their crankiness at each other, only the spinster Doris goes over the edge, at one point threatening to "staple [Doreen's] tits together" (*GF* 13). Doris's irritability has made her a difficult colleague. Because work means more to her than to her younger, married office mate, an innocent comment about office procedure can raise her hackles. Answering Doreen's friendly suggestion that she learn computer technology, Doris accuses Doreen of wanting to get rid of her (*GF* 6).

Does her accusation have any merit? By omitting the name of the firm for which the women work along with the product or service the firm provides, Bennett calls attention to such questions. Doreen Bidmead, "a married lady in her thirties" (*GF* 1), would like to rise in the firm. She insists that, although classified a Grade 4, she has been doing the work of a Grade 3; moreover, she would already have been promoted had the central office not frozen all rankings. She doth protest too much. Friendship between semiskilled colleagues in England during the recession of the late 1970s faced big hurdles. Doris, imagining the specter of redundancy drifting into view, comforts herself with her Grade 3 ranking; her seniority will protect her from being fired. Doreen will retort that only a quirk in personnel policy stands between her and Doris in the firm's hierarchy. Yet she also knows that Doris outranks her; any decision to eliminate one of the jobs in the office the two women share will leave Doreen redundant.

But it would not leave her crushed. "That's the thing about marriage, there's always two of you" (*GF* 3), Doreen reminds her senior coworker in one of several point-scoring maneuvers she performs in the play. She ignores Doris's reply, "There's two of Mother and me" (*GF* 3), in favor of citing her Clifford's options if an economic slump left him jobless. The sole bread-winner in her home, Doris lacks these options, as both women know. Thus their duel with invisible swords is prolonged. Min-utes after hearing Doreen's reference to the consolations of mar-riage, Doris says of a colleague, "She's probably been sacked. . . . Wasn't she your grade" (*GF* 7)? No winner emerges from the protracted verbal joust. Doreen's job means less to her than her home. Doris, conversely, has invested more of herself in the firm because she needs work routine more than Doreen does; also, the office provides her with a paycheck, with the self-validation that comes from feeling useful, with some social out-lets, and with time away from her mother. No wonder the shadow cast by Dorothy Binns upsets her. Though Doris would prob-ably trade life situations with Doreen, given the chance, Doreen would never choose to walk in Doris's sensible shoes.

This reluctance would be based on direct observation. It comes out piecemeal that the two women have been working together for some time. Their bond is neither thin nor shallow.

They have devised little rituals to help both standardize and evaluate their workaday routine. These rituals have brought them closer. Doris's mother has made some towels for Doreen without ever having met her, and Doreen protects Doris from an unwanted phone caller during the course of the action (*GF* 5). Yet the women also grate on each other. They can act more like feuding sisters than like office mates. Nor will their rivalry end. They attack each other's weak spots; they quarrel over trifles; they fight dirty rather than yield ground. But they also stand up for each other to outsiders. A moment after Doreen tells Doris to stop talking, Lomax enters the office with a clipboard. Seeing Doreen's tearful face, he asks her what's wrong. But Doris intervenes: "It's nothing. Her mother-in-law's poorly" (*GF* 22). Doris cannot stop Lomax from gossiping as he moves from office to office. But she can prevent him from babbling about her spats with Doreen.

The destroyer in both of the scripts comprising *Office Suite* is a woman. This is no oddity. Deprived for decades from holding top-level jobs in business, women gravitated into the fields of social and health services. Then changes in the industrial West after World War II gave them more power than they had ever dreamed of enjoying. As business has moved away from the production of material goods in favor of the processing and disseminating of information, women have been filling still more space in the executive suite.

Bennett's recently retired Arthur Dodsworth seems untouched by this upheaval. He also stands light years away from Old Testament patriarchs like Job and Abraham, whose harshest trials come in old age. He is coasting and enjoying it. He has been sorely tried, the recent past having set him the ordeals of adjusting to both his wife Winnie's death and retirement. But he has adjusted well. His bowling, his Rotary meetings, his classes in both cooking and pottery making, and the visits of his grand-children fill as much of his time as he wants filled. Which is not all that much; he also enjoys dozing in his soft, warm armchair and talking to his pet budgie. This cozy regimen ends with the unannounced appearance at his door of his former secretary, the eponym of *A Visit from Miss Prothero* (1978). Bennett's most vicious character, Peggy Prothero unleashes her malevolence straightaway. She has not taken a day of vacation or sick leave to visit her old boss. In fact, she has never taken an unscheduled day off during her whole stay at Warburtons; she even returned to the office the afternoon of her mother's funeral "to do the backlog" (*Visit* 3). Peggy visits Dodsworth on a day when Warburtons is closed for its annual staff picnic, which she is not attending. She has also come with a purpose. Wretched herself, she wants to crush joy and peace wherever she can find them.

What is so riveting and frightening about *Visit* is the ease with which she succeeds. This one-act companion piece to *Green Forms* depicts the fragility of happiness. Dodsworth's success-ful adjustment to his new routine is shattered within half an hour by a harpy about whom he has no illusions. When she is in the bathroom, out of earshot, he mutters, "get off home, you bad, boring bitch" (*Visit* 8). But he is too much the gentleman to send her away. A good host in addition to being likeable, decent, and benevolent, he serves his unwanted guest coffee and cake. Per-haps his kind heart stops him from seeing that she has come to him bearing poison. Immediately, she jockeys to gain an edge over him. Rather than asking whether she has disturbed him, she lets him know, while entering his living room without being asked, that he kept her waiting at the door a minute or two. She keeps him off balance. Fussy, overly formal, and mindful of her dignity, she wants to set the tone for the coming exchange with Dodsworth. She keeps her coat on until invited to remove it. Neither will she sit till asked. Later, she rebukes him for his hospitality. His offer of a cup of tea shocks her. "Tea? With my kidneys?" she asks, comparing its effect on her system to that of hydrochloric acid, as if he should know her medical history (*Visit* 7). But he is not alone in letting her down. Her discontent covers a wide range, including the food in the firm's canteen, a coworker's eczema, and a secretary who has been circulating photos of her out-of-wedlock child around the office.

The main target of Peggy's spite, though, is Dodsworth. She calls the clock he got four months earlier an inappropriate gift for a retiree, phrasing her cavil in terms as hurtful as she can make them: "Time dribbling away and nothing to look forward to. Tick-tock-tick-tock. It would get on my nerves" (*Visit* 9). Her determination to rasp his nerves holds steady. After hearing that the cake being served to her was baked by Dodsworth's daughter, she asks for a smaller slice than good manners might call for. Later, this shrew who holds others to such strict accounts refers to Dodsworth's dead wife Winnie as "Millie," which is the name of his pet budgie. Perhaps she wants him to ponder the possibility that Millie has become his substitute wife or, still worse, that she is better company for him than Winnie was.

Such an innuendo would be in character for Peggy, a wretch who finds ways to avoid dispensing simple humanity. She pretends to be baffled by the ashtray Dodsworth made in pottery class, she winces at the news that he is learning to cook, and she calls the dress that Winnie wore in the Dodsworths' wedding picture "Funny" (*Visit* 4). But these light hits are merely intended to soften Dodsworth for the heavy artillery she has come to bombard him with. The stated purpose of her visit is to update him on what has been going on at the firm where he worked for thirty years. But this purpose has a stinger in its tail. His claim that the leisure he has been enjoying since his retirement has swept Warburtons from his thoughts does not faze her. He still retains a residual interest in his old firm, as she knows. And she hopes to stir up this residue. She begins by explaining how his successor has been expanding the firm's client base to include places like Zambia, Japan, and Rumania. This expansion has produced side effects, she adds. While strengthening Warburtons' profit potential, Mr. Skinner's marketing policies have also done away with the long-standing camaraderie that made the firm such a jolly work environment. Replacing the casualness that prevailed during Dodsworth's watch is a new tightness of discipline. The jokes that once adorned the office walls have all come down, and colleagues have stopped calling each other by their first names.

Now Dodsworth accepts the inevitability of change, at least in principle. Letting on that he resents the direction Warburtons has been taking since his retirement not only makes him look curmudgeonly but also shows that Peggy has tricked him into talking like both a hypocrite and a foe of progress. Is he doddering into obsolescence, he wonders. To recoup lost ground, he shows Peggy a chart depicting interoffice procedures he devised in 1947. He calls the connections depicted on the chart "basically . . . the same set-up as we've got today" (*Visit* 13). Peggy jumps on his mistake. Timing her hits with an Iago-like cunning, she tells him that all the procedures and policies he brought about have been scrapped and supplanted by better ones. Acting as a reluctant bearer of bad news, she comes close to saying that Dodsworth's retirement has helped Warburtons thrive. Since he left, filing has been computerized and a new billing system has halved the time it took to match receipts and invoices in Dodsworth's day. The firm is thus grossing more money than ever.

Peggy knows that being told about the dismantling of his work will sting Dodsworth, who invested a great deal of himself in Warburtons. Hearing that the firm has benefited from disposing of the system he spent four years phasing in makes him feel puny and inconsequential. Peggy has accomplished her mission. She has made him doubt that he left anything of value behind him; thirty years of effort have been drained of meaning. But why has she selected him as the object of her malice? Some of her behavior defies explanation.

Perhaps Peggy wants to see Dodsworth, who is probably the same age as her incapacitated father, dumped in a home. But he would be punished for his fidelity, not his unfaithfulness. Her last words in the play, "Well, we always had a soft spot for one another you and me, didn't we?" (*Visit* 18), suggest that she had an unrequited crush on him all the years they worked together. His age may not have ruled out an attraction to him any more than her father's limp discouraged *his* many sexual conquests. Perhaps she threw Dodsworth's obsolescence in his face because she has no other way of punishing the father who may have included her in the "droves" (*Visit* 11) of women he deceived his wife with.

A history of forbidden romantic involvements beginning with one at the family hearth could well explain Peggy's maladjustment. And maladjusted she is. What appears to have been a run-in at Warburtons' previous year's picnic has kept her away from this year's event. She has no regrets. This thin-skinned woman who clashes with her colleagues can feel satisfied with her day's work; besides rattling Dodsworth, she has lowered his self-esteem. Yet she will never pound him down to her level. As is shown in his flair for cooking and pottery, he enjoys challenges. He is also resilient and adaptive. Though badly shaken, he will get over the trauma caused by Peggy's visit. She, however, is trapped in her awfulness, and soon she will run out of possible victims. The similarities between her and Dodsworth have made him an easy target for her poison. They used to work together. Now they are both outsiders. But he misses the picnic by choice. She stays away because she feels she must. Her options are shrinking. Persona non grata among her coworkers, she will soon deplete her store of ex-colleagues. Then she will face the horrors of isolation. Bennett invites this outcome while avoiding lyrical, highly polished dialogue in favor of the plainspokenness of the industrial North.

CHAPTER FIVE

Spies and Other Exiles

The alternation in Bennett's writing between home and work and also between a cheerful acceptance of change and the doggedness of his conservative North-of-England roots can mask his imaginative intent. Despite having written in *An Englishman Abroad, A Question of Attribution,* and *The Old Country,* three plays about Englishmen of privilege who gave classified secrets to the USSR during the cold war, Bennett has disclaimed what looks like an ongoing interest in spies and spying. This disclaimer makes good sense. His statement in *Objects of Affection* (217) that exile concerns him much more than espionage chimes with his fascination for Kafka, the archetypal nonbelonger of the century. Kafka taught him that a sense of exile and displacement can afflict those who live with their families while holding full-time jobs in their hometowns. This alienation can also stalk Bennett's people when they leave the nest to go on vacation. Their discomfort is both funny and sad, often because they cannot explain it, convinced as they are that they are leading blameless lives and that they are in all ways as upright as their neighbors. These people deserve sympathy. Besides living in an England beset with economic woes, they have seen the reputation of their country's security network collapse in the international intelligence community because of the ease with which top-level spies like Kim Philby, Guy Burgess, and Donald Maclean turned restricted information over to the Soviets and then flew to Moscow without a glance, let alone a restraining hand, from the British Secret Service.

These traitors' freedom of movement created another situation Bennett found both funny and sad. But as compatible as it is with his comic impulse, he prefers to use it as a backdrop against which he projects the plight of the exile. This plight he treats without condescension or sentimentality. And, rather than defining exile politically, he shows what a traitor like Guy Burgess shares with a jobless householder from Leeds on vacation with his family or with an Asian trying to learn English while waiting tables in Scarborough.

I

Like *All Day on the Sands,* which also first played on London Weekend Television in February 1979, *Afternoon Off* takes as its main setting a resort hotel. But it differs from its companion piece in focusing on the hotel staffers rather than on the guests. The main character of the telescript, in which both Pete Postlethwaite and Bennett had parts, is an Asian waiter named Lee. In his introduction to *The Writer in Disguise,* which includes *Afternoon Off,* Bennett calls Lee "the ineffectual hero taken to a logical conclusion . . . lying in his underpants staring at the ceiling" (*WD* 9) in the script's next-to-last scene. Lee's status as a writer in disguise evokes his lonely quest for a goal that keeps drifting in and out of view, causing both his energy and his self-confidence to waver and flag.

His race brings out the worst traits of his adoptive townsfolk. A hotel cook claims apropos of Lee that Asians "don't set much store by human life" (*WD* 226), an opinion that meshes well with the reaction of a coffee-shop owner who sees him crying: "I didn't think they did cry. I thought that was the point about them" (*WD* 250). The art gallery attendant played by Postlethwaite believes Lee a lowlife who has come to the gallery not to look at the paintings but to enjoy the central heating. Even Lee's acts of kindness backfire: despite having done nothing wrong, he is ejected from three places during the hour-long teleplay. Having been mistakenly directed to an elderly hospital patient whom nobody visits, he finally encounters someone lonelier and more trapped than himself. But another visitor insults him when she is trying to compliment him, insisting that the Dairy Box chocolates he gave Old Iris were made by Japanese who pasted the English label on the box. Old Iris herself cites the chocolates' "funny taste" (*WD* 254). Then a West Indian staff nurse who enters the ward savages Lee for giving the diabetic Old Iris candy, which could put her in a coma for the second time that week.

What wears Lee down is the frustration he keeps facing in his quest; he need not speak good English to feel the sting of other people's contempt. The lure of love inspired his quest. Early on, he had told a fellow waiter named Bernard that he wanted to meet a young English woman. Bernard tried to help him. He said that a local woman named Iris saw his passport photo and was charmed by his olive skin. Full of purpose and tenacity, Lee spends his afternoon off looking for her. The thoroughness of his search gives Bennett a chance to survey the Yorkshire vacation town of Scarborough. Moving from a hotel kitchen to an art gallery, a couple of churches, a hospital, a shoe store, and then a factory, the search provides revealing looks at people differing in age, social background, and educational level. But Bennett finds unity amid this diversity, not only at Lee's expense. The trait shared by most of Lee's new neighbors is a readiness to profit at the expense of others. A saleswoman claims that a shoe that squeezes a customer's foot fits perfectly because she wants to make a sale, and the store has no shoes of the proper size in stock. Iris's father, Duggie, who has learned to be wary of others, thinks Lee is either a pimp or a drug dealer. Cyril, a benevolent coworker, tries to curb Duggie's wrath by saying that Lee "might be a nice lad." Duggie's retort, "You wouldn't be saying that if he came sniffing round your Christine," serves as a reminder that Christine may have been sniffing round Lee (*WD* 246). A receptionist named Christine referred to his "nice face" (*WD* 241) and directed him to the printing shop where Duggie works with the lower-class expression, "come on, love" (*WD* 243).

Were this receptionist and Cyril's Christine the same person, the solicitude she extends to Lee might have easily rankled her father. This rancor would have meshed with the teleplay's logic. Lee's search for Iris causes trouble wildly disproportionate to the innocent goodwill with which it is conducted. Though Lee finds out Iris's last name in the shoe store where she once worked, he also learns that she was fired for theft. Then he is asked to leave the store. His presence in the factory where Iris's father works has made Duggie relive the grief and rage Iris roused in him before he disowned her and banished her from his home. Then, predictably enough, Duggie's boss ejects Lee from the factory, less upset by the stir he has caused than by the possibility that the City Council sent him to inspect the factory's fire precaution system.

One can understand why Lee reels out of the shop thinking that England has gone mad. His prospects, though, may be brighter in this madhouse than he believes. Like Kafka of *Kafka's*

Dick and Franz of *The Insurance Man,* he attracts women. In addition to Christine, a flower arranger in a church offered him companionship and kindness, which he rejected in favor of looking for Iris. Then a saleswoman in the shoe store where Iris once worked "looks sympathetically at him" (*WD* 236), writes on a piece of paper the name of the factory where Duggie works, and hints that she would enjoy his company. Finally, a hospital patient in her sixties says Lee has "nice hair" (*WD* 252). She is probably the only one of this quartet of admiring women who would not suit him better than Duggie's Iris, who shrinks in both stature and moral character as the script moves ahead. Iris is working now as a nurse's aide, or "hospital skivvy," in her father's words, "emptying slops, cleaning out bedpans": Duggie could be on target with his claim that this drudgery is "all she's fit for" (*WD* 247). Like Dorothy Binns of *Green Forms,* Iris shows up only at the very end of a Bennett play whose plot revolves around her. But she lacks Ms. Binns's harsh puritanism. She is in bed with Bernard, the hotel waiter who said she wanted to meet Lee. In the corner of Bernard's room stands a pair of gaudy boots, the theft of which probably cost her her last job. Lee deserves better than Iris.

Yet his efforts to find her cannot be scorned as a waste. The play's last scene shows him back on the job; he has survived his setback with Iris. Also worth noting along with this resiliency is his persistence. Until he traces Iris to the hospital, talismanic box of chocolates in hand, he lets nothing distract him from his quest. Perhaps the quest means more to him than Iris, its object. The same grit that restores him to work the morning after his disastrous afternoon off riveted him to his purpose. He was not deterred by the discovery that theft cost her two jobs any more than he was by her father's denunciation of her. Of course, it is possible that he lacks the English to take in Duggie's meaning. But he must have caught the general drift of Duggie and her other detractors. Perhaps he is so lonely that he is willing to overlook Iris's failings. Ironically, this charity, like the purity of his knightly quest, proves his superiority over Iris. He need not concede so much to move close to woman. Women do like him.

But he needs to find one to click with, and it is not clear that he will. *Afternoon Off* bristles with such imponderables. Is Christine kindly Cyril's daughter? Is Lee the first name or the last name of the play's main figure? Again on the subject of names, often a preoccupation with Bennett, why is one of the male cooks at the hotel where Lee works called Marjory? Perhaps an answer to such questions lies somewhere along the edge of a minor character's choice of a name for a coffee house she runs: "It's called the Pop In because . . . you know that's what people do . . . just pop in . . . except old Geoff says it's called Pop In because Pop's always in, which he is, he has to . . . look after the place. . . . He's actually out just this minute, popped along to the bank, popped in there, ha ha" (*WD* 249). Jane's recitation shows that things can have more than one meaning; Lee meets two Irises before locating the one he spent several hours searching for. Yet seeing him in person moves her less than looking at his picture. Also puzzling is why she would go to bed with Bernard after Bernard encouraged Lee to seek her out. She must have changed her mind about both men. The play abounds in both misconnections and failures to connect, mostly because of problems in vision like Iris's. Just as Lee allows the energy he pours into his quest for Iris to cloud his perception of her worth, so do the people he meets during the quest misjudge *him*. He no more ruined Iris's life with drugs, as her father suspects (*WD* 246), than he is a fire marshal or the walking bundle of racial clichés by which some of his new neighbors in Scarborough explain him.

But if the perceiver, or subject, miscues, the object, or person, being perceived, will miss out on the justice he/she deserves. A hospital patient links her belief that Lee is Japanese to the Japanese car her son owns (*WD* 252). Fond of associations, she then yokes her first name, Daisy, to that of the florally named Iris. This association carries forward: "All we want now is a Buttercup and we'd be a right bunch" (*WD* 252). Maybe they are already a right bunch. Iris's last name may not be Buttercup, but it comes close enough at Butterfield. The data comprising *Afternoon Off* either graze each other or mirror each other suggestively. How to grasp their meaning? The pattern of counterimages and dovetailings governing the play suggests a deep interconnectedness perhaps more accessible to Asian passiveness than to Western pragmatism. But the play's lone Asian is also its busiest character. Besides tracking the missing person Iris with the dedication of a fictional private eye, Lee has already met the challenges of coming to the UK, finding work, and learning some English. These exertions make him more Western than any of the Westerners in the teleplay. He probably also underrates his ability to attract women. The doggedness with which he defies audience expectations shows that Bennett intended *Afternoon Off* as a blueprint for dealing with reality. Much of the challenge of perceiving Lee correctly stems from cultural clichés that have seeped into the public domain. But if Bennett is more of a goad than a polemicist, he also reveals, in his arresting, involving script, a knack for stirring controversy at several important levels.

II

The Guy Burgess created by Bennett in *An Englishman Abroad* (1988) is shabby, smelly, and "running to seed" (*SS* 1) because of a surfeit of alcohol. A hard drinker most of his adult life, this ex-Foreign Office chief has been boozing more than ever since his defection to the Soviet Union five years before the time the play unfolds. The well-cut English suit he had on during his 1953 flight to Moscow has become scuffed and frayed as a result of his many drunken spills. Furthermore, his public image has faded and shrunk. He is rarely mentioned, let alone discussed, in Britain. He is faring still worse in his grotty new home. In the months following his arrival in Moscow, he enjoyed celebrity and perhaps some notoriety. Besides being denied phone calls and mail from home, he fell under the constant scrutiny of the Kremlin's top intelligencers. Now, his only watcher is a sixteen-year-old trainee. Posterity may rub him out completely, he worries, so often is he linked to Donald Maclean, the other turncoat with whom he flew to Moscow in what a British embassy worker calls, in the telescript of *An Englishman Abroad,* "an unfortunate elopement" (*OA* 232). Being denied the singularity of existence is rankling enough on its own to Burgess. But he does not like Maclean and never spends time with him despite being starved for English-language conversation.

"Actually, there's no one in Moscow at all. It's like staying up in Cambridge for the Long Vac. One makes do with whoever's around" (*SS* 6), he says of the drabness and desolation of his Moscow exile. Besides filling in hours of idle time, he has to reinvent himself every day, networking in the shadow of the KGB. Thus he prizes the visit of real-life actress Coral Browne to Moscow with the Stratford Memorial Theatre Group. So grungy and lowdown is he that he steals soap, cigarettes, face powder, and whisky from her dressing room. So reckless is he that he assumes that she will excuse his crime. This assumption is important to him. For what he wants more than the oddments he steals is the chance to gossip about home. Bennett's Burgess belies the popular image of the traitor just as Lee of *Afternoon Off* did that of the Asian. He likes the *Times* crossword puzzle, quotes *Tristram Shandy* and Robert Browning, admires the novels of Jane Austen and Trollope, and sings old hymns. No Spartan, he enjoys luxury, nuzzling the velvety pile of Coral's fur coat after she enters his squalid flat.

Sentimentality and nostalgia also run high with this Judas. The 1982 telescript has him saying the Russian equivalent of *Où sont les neiges d'antan?* (Where are the snows of yesteryear?) (*OA* 238). Burgess tells Coral, "I can say I love London. I can say I love England. But I can't say I love my country. I don't know what that means" (*SS* 9). If his boozy puzzlement does mean anything, it probably refers to his discontent with postcolonial Britain's dependence on the United States in the decade after World War II, with Britain's huge, spongy espionage industry, and with the country's dullness—neither the discovery of North Sea oil nor the Beatles-induced Carnaby Street fashion revolution having yet occurred. But what if they had? Would they not have offended the mandarin tastes Burgess acquired at Eton and Cambridge? He has no illusions about the USSR, calling the "pigsty" where he lives, "By their standards . . . quite commodious. Palatial even. One is very lucky" (*SS* 4). Then he complains about the wretchedness of Russian clothing, dentistry, and conversation. Perhaps Burgess cannot even explain his reasons for betraying Britain. He does cite the Soviet system and says of his treachery, "It seemed the right thing to do at the time" (*SS* 9, 10). But these words, lacking the support of concrete references, are too lame to justify his deceit.

He takes refuge in irony. But he has carried irony to the point where it has recoiled on itself, distorting those contrarian impulses in him that drew him to treason. This inveterate gossip asks Coral only about Englishmen who are either homosexual like himself or bisexual—E. M. Forster, W. H. Auden, and Cyril Connolly. He even mentions an actor he directed at Cambridge who played a woman's role in drag (SS 5). No agent of violent change, he listens only to the countering mentality that rules him. In some ways, he is the play's most predictable, conventional figure. This alleged promoter of the overthrow of Western society says of London in the telescript of *An Englishman Abroad,* "I don't want it to change. Why does anybody want to change it? They've no business changing it. The fools" (*OA* 241). Yet he always undermined the heritage he claims to prize. Though he lived in a chic Jermyn Street flat, he neglected it so badly that he ran it down to the squalor of his Moscow pigsty. Were he still in London, he would find plenty to complain about. Distance is a function of enchantment for this foe of the convenient and the available. One of his first questions to Coral concerns a long-forgotten music hall comedy team which used to appear on the radio. Like many other exiles, he clings desperately to the signs and norms of his ex-homeland's past.

But this puffy-faced, shabbily dressed traitor who speaks with such cultivated nonchalance may be exerting more self-control than Coral first thinks. He wastes no energy straining against the shackles his Soviet hosts have imposed on him. He plays his piano. He has evolved a tender, loving relationship with the young man he lives with. Valuing the human contact Tolya provides, he does not worry whether his live-in lover was assigned to watch him by the KGB. Burgess deserves Coral's attention. He has managed to survive in dreary, underprovisioned Moscow despite both his loneliness and his unspoken contempt for the bankrupt ideology that brought him there. If anything, his exile has made him more English than he was at home. He craves gossip about his old social set for the *pukka sahib* off-handedness in which the gossip is couched as much as for its content. He and Tolya also play a Gilbert and Sullivan tune together. Finally, he misses his mother.

The only thing he can count on in his bedraggled police state is himself. He knows he has abused that self. But as degraded as he has become, he nonetheless clings to those scraps of selfhood that have survived decades of maltreatment. And now he wants to recover from these frayed scraps some of his bygone English elegance. "I don't want to look like everybody else" *SS* (6), he says to justify his asking Coral to order him a custom-made suit in London. There's something bogus as well as pathetic in his request. He wants to celebrate the same Englishness he betrayed by giving top-level military secrets to his country's enemy.

Coral understands both his hypocrisy and his pathos. She also remembers that he had feigned sickness in her dressing room in order to pinch the wares she had brought to Moscow with her from England. Nor will she excuse his misconduct: "you pissed in our soup and we drank it" (*SS* 10), she says of his spying and defection, violating the well-bred English practice of sidestepping conflict. Though his public school manner has set the tone for their exchange, it has not erased his guilt. Coral flouts etiquette and decorum for two reasons. First, she wants Burgess to know that his shopworn charm has not fooled her. Next, she holds little brief with English breeding and taste because she is Australian. But her Australianness takes a different turn from what Burgess had expected. She is no wide-eyed colonial ready to cave in to his well-bred public school man's nonchalance. Yield she does, but because she has tasted enough of exile herself to want to brighten the squalid isolation he opted for.

So Coral does order him a suit at a bespoke London clothier (along with a hat in the television version). But a salesclerk in another shop refuses to sell her pajamas for Burgess's use. This rebuff leads to the play's dramatic climax. The shop, Coral reminds the clerk, has always done business with adulterers, and it did not turn Burgess away when much of London knew him as "one of the most notorious buggers in London and a drunkard in the bargain. Only then he was in the Foreign Office" (*SS* 13), she adds, citing a connection that excused his guilt. Her Australian twang pushing to the fore as her moral indignation mounts, she ends her diatribe with a plea for freedom of belief: "the gentleman in question has shown himself to have some principles, principles which aren't yours and, as a matter of interest, aren't mine" (*SS* 14). Does Burgess deserve to be punished for acting on beliefs that oppose the prevailing English code of apathy and compliance? "Thank Christ I'm not English" (*SS* 14), she concludes.

And anyone seated in the auditorium who cheered her attack on English conformity and complacency would have flushed with embarrassment at this point. Coral's broadside carries limited force because she delivers it while standing on shaky ground. The salesclerk's polite disclosure that his firm is not English but Hungarian pads the moral jolt of her outburst. A 1956 anticommunist revolution in Hungary brought Soviet tanks and troops into Budapest a scant two or three years before Coral's visit to the Hungarian-owned haberdashery; 60,000 locals were killed, including the prime minister. Why would the haberdashery want a Soviet apparatchik as a customer, even if he spoke BBC English? Codalike, each of the play's last two scenes rises to a climax that is then punctured. Burgess is last seen looking "the picture of an English gentleman" with his natty new garb, umbrella, and cigarette holder (*SS* 14). Enforcing this elegance is a concert version of Gilbert and Sullivan's "For He Is an Englishman," from *H.M.S. Pinafore,* with full chorus and orchestra, filling the house. Yet this impression is not the play's last: Bennett segues from this triumphant multisensory glimpse of Burgess to Coral. More than fifteen years have passed since her Moscow visit. Referring to the 1982 telecast of *An Englishman Abroad* (*WH* 214), Coral recounts her talk with a Foreign Office minister who told her that Burgess could probably have returned to the UK to visit his aged, ailing mother without being indicted for treason. This disclosure jars Coral. Now dead, Burgess had approached her in Moscow to use her. Use her he did, as well as make her feel foolish. But she understood and forgave him. At play's end, she needs some forgiveness and understanding herself.

Only the 1988 stage version of *Englishman* ended with Coral's troubled reminiscence. The telescript shows Burgess (1911–63) walking unaccompanied in his finery down a Moscow street with the *Pinafore* tune rising to a crescendo as the action ends. Alan Bates's Burgess is the last person to appear on screen. This solo apparition was foreshadowed by the work's opening scene. On the stage of the Moscow Art Theater, Claudius is addressing Rosenkrantz and Guildenstern in act 2, scene 2, of *Hamlet.* He speaks of the shocking change that has taken place in Hamlet since his return to Elsinore: "nor the exterior nor the inward man / Resembles that it was" (*OA* 221), he explains to the prince's old friends. Burgess's smart new togs sharply change his "exterior." But the external improvement has not altered his inward man. Yes, he has avoided being absorbed by his surroundings. But by spying for the Soviets while working in the Foreign Office in London, he had done roughly the same thing. Is there anything more to him than a drive to reject his immediate milieu, a drive that may merely be the ironist's fear of commitment? (Burgess calls himself a "coward" [*SS* 3].)

Such questions count with Bennett. But he shrinks from judging in favor of inciting debate over the moral and political issues his play has invited. He sympathizes neither with Burgess nor with the homeland he betrayed. A hint of the neutrality he observes appears in the play's introduction: "I find it hard to drum up any public indignation over Burgess," Bennett said in 1982 (*OA* 219). But this equanimity reflects the same exaggerated irony he attributes to Burgess himself. Either Bennett is being too generous or he is twisting the facts to create a blueprint for his Brechtian drama of alienation. His introduction contrasts Kim Philby, whose divulgences to the Kremlin sent British troops to "torture and death," with the allegedly "silly" indiscretions of Burgess, which only came to making "fools of people in high places" (*OA* 219). Like Philby and Maclean, Burgess was a communist mole in the executive branch of British Intelligence. Told by Philby that they were facing arrest, Burgess and Maclean left England in a manner staged to discredit the Special Branch—Bennett's "people in high places."

Not only were the two traitors allowed to flee the country while under investigation; of special embarrassment to Whitehall was the publication of the news that Maclean had been arrested earlier for drunkenness and street brawling and that Burgess had a police record for homosexuality, drunk driving, illegal entry, and assault and battery. That these two Soviet spies had been vetted by London's top security officers raised global doubt concerning the British government's ability to protect its citizens.

As an autonomous art object, *Englishman* does not suffer from the anti-British feeling that dictated its composition. The variety of settings in the telecast creates a rich, detailed picture of Moscow in the early years of the Thaw, following Stalin's death. Whereas the stage version is sullen and grim, like Moscow itself, the mobility of the television camera contrasts this gloom with London's glitter, thereby creating one of the play's leading motifs together with the reminder of Burgess's nagging anxiety that he erred, to begin with, by leaguing with the Soviets. The small screen also depicts the bustle and sparkle of backstage life between the acts of a play and, in the telescript's outdoor scenes, the Muscovites' collective fear of being caught fraternizing with or giving information to foreigners. Besides being discouraged by British Embassy staffers from lunching with Burgess, Coral gets little help from the pedestrians she asks to direct her to Burgess's flat.

The single bifurcating root that joins the people never emerges. But perhaps it is hinted at. One cannot ignore the ease with which Burgess's petty thievery incites criminal motives in Coral, who steals a tape measure from her theater group's wardrobe master to measure Burgess for his suit of clothes. Then there is the script's aggressive toilet imagery. After telling Burgess, "you pissed in our soup and we drank it" (*SS* 10), Coral spews even harsher invective at the London salesclerk who refuses to sell her pajamas: "And perhaps if you'd be gracious enough to lower your trousers, Mr. Burgess, we could be privileged enough to thrust our tongue between the cheeks of your arse" (*SS* 13), she says in a parody of the deference the clerk would have extended Burgess before his defection despite having known of his debauchery. Such moments place the point of convergence between Bennett's people at a lower level than their witty, stylish backchat might suggest. By challenging popular assumptions about social dynamics, *Englishman* puts theatergoers at greater risk than they might have expected when the house lights started to dim. Like Pirandello and Brecht before him, Bennett has shown one of the main functions of stage drama to consist of casting fresh light on our ethics and thus prodding us to reexamine how we live.

III

Anthony Blunt (1907–83) may have been, after Roger Fry, England's greatest art historian, attaining eminence as an authority on seventeenth-century painting, particularly that of Nicolas Poussin. In homage to his distinction, Blunt was named surveyor of the king's (later the queen's) pictures and director of the Courtauld Institute. This prestige helped him in another way—as cover. While studying at Cambridge in the 1930s, he had come under the influence of Guy Burgess, a force that persisted after his graduation. As an officer in British Intelligence during World War II, Blunt gave classified secrets to the Soviets. Then he helped set up the 1951 London-to-Moscow flight of Burgess and Maclean. The British Secret Service had discovered Blunt's disloyalty by 1964 but, rather than arresting him, started using him as an informer. Not until 1979 was he denounced as the mysterious "fourth man" in the spy ring consisting of Burgess, Maclean, and Philby. Soon afterward, he was stripped of the knighthood awarded him in 1956.

A fourth and even a fifth man both appear in an X-ray photo of the portrait *Titian and a Venetian Senator,* which was known as the *Triple Portrait* after a third figure was discovered in it some centuries before the fourth and fifth figures were found. The Titian canvas is still called the *Triple Portrait,* which is why Bennett made it so central to his play *A Question of Attribution*

(1988). When Blunt tells a visitor that he is living two lives, he is corrected. The visitor puts the number at three in one of the many likenesses the play teases out between art and espionage. Asked by a palace footman to summarize an impromptu conversation with Queen Elizabeth II, Blunt says, "I was talking about art. I'm not sure that she was" (*SS* 51).

Another painting central to the theme of *A Question of Attribution* is also by Titian (1477–1576) and is called the *Allegory of Prudence* (*SS* 22). Bennett may have been drawn to this work because it includes three men, one of whom looks just like the third man discovered standing to the side in the *Triple Portrait*. This figure represents maturity. Titian's three allegorical subjects stand for youth, maturity, and old age or what Erwin Panofsky (whom Bennett cites in his note) calls "memory, intelligence, and foresight, and the latter's subordination to the concept of prudence."[1] The painting's "motto," if it has one, says Panofsky, is this: "From the [experience of the] past, the present acts prudently, lest it spoil future action" (149). This interpretation applies to Blunt, whose treachery has robbed him of both options and time. A drama of ripe condition, *Question* depicts his last hours before his arrest by the British Secret Service.

Like Ibsen's Hedda Gabler and Tennessee Williams's Blanche Dubois, two other doomed souls, he knows that his sole option lies in controlling the style of his leave-taking. But the stoicism he tries to maintain keeps slipping a gear. "People find me cold" (*SS* 29), he tells a restorer in the play's first scene. Then the mysterious Chubb, who knows more about him than anyone else in the play, says, "you work rather hard at being a cold fish" (*SS* 34). Chubb also appreciates how much Blunt sweats to look cold: "you must always be on tenterhooks, frightened to put a foot wrong, having to watch every word" (*SS* 34). Chubb's words strike home, because Blunt has been struggling to keep his poise in the shadow of disaster. While lecturing on Giovanni Bellini's (ca. 1430–1516) *Agony in the Garden,* Blunt cites the absence of agony in Renaissance portrayals of martyrdom: "these martyrs seldom lose a drop of their sang-froid, so cool about their bizarre torments. . . . About suffering they were always wrong, the Old Masters" (*SS* 30). This paraphrase of Auden takes root in Blunt's own psyche. Martyrdom is on his mind. But the comforting parallel he tries to tease out between religious art and spying has eluded him. In serving the Kremlin, he threw in with liars, cheats, and thugs. And he will soon have to divulge the details of this shameful compact, a hard chore because everybody despises a traitor, even those whom his treachery has helped. Suffering awaits Blunt, and he knows it.

While waiting to explain himself, he finds solace in the ruse of moving his treachery into the aesthetic sphere, stripping it of moral content. This ruse automatically makes his deceit a lapse of taste or an indiscretion rather than a crime. Performing a mental acrobatic that may have been inspired by the art critic Panofsky (159), Blunt tends to cloud and complicate the simple rather than clarifying the difficult and the obscure, which is the job of all teachers. In one of those statements that bear upon both art history and spying, he tells the queen (who is referred to in Bennett's text as "HMQ"), "Because something is not what it is said to be, ma'am, does not mean it's a fake. It may just have been wrongly attributed" (*SS* 44). A copy of an Old Master, he claims, though not an original, may have some intrinsic worth. Accordingly, the sleuth-hounds from British Intelligence may be wasting their time by stalking him. He has done nothing wrong except perhaps to flout good form. And even if he did perpetrate a crime, he did it with the appropriate elegance and erudition. His preference for the convoluted over the simple has elevated slime and sleaze into something grand. And grandeur is his bailiwick. He is, after all, a member of the queen's household, an eminence he would have never attained were he not a man of breeding and refinement.

Weak as it is, this self-justification comforts Blunt until his exchange with HMQ near the end of the one-act play. *New York Times* drama critic Frank Rich was thinking of that exchange, one of the sharpest Bennett ever wrote, in speaking of the multileveled richness of the playwright's dialogue: "While the dialogue's surface is often in the third-person diction of the British Establishment, its subtext is aflame with subversive innuendo."[2] The exchange starts with a brilliant sight gag. Blunt is speaking from a ladder to two juniors about a painting when HMQ strolls onto the set. Awed by her, the young men politely leave. But Blunt, who has been looking at a painting while addressing them, continues his impromptu lecture. When he is not handed the magnifying glass he has been asking for, he grows impatient. "Come along—we haven't all day" (*SS* 43), he carps. He receives the glass after a pause, but he is still cranky. After descending to floor level, he chides the absent young men for failing to steady his ladder: "I could have fallen on my face," he grumps. HMQ's rejoinder, "I think you already have," spoken from the spot vacated by the young men, stuns him (*SS* 44). He does not regain his lost balance and composure during the exchange that follows. Alert, inquisitive, and well informed on a variety of topics, HMQ has not dissolved inside her ceremonial function. She avoids using the royal *we,* relying on her presence rather than her office to declare her nobility.

And Bennett sides with her. Writing with respect, he betrays no need to stand above her or to show her committing a gaffe. She remains in charge. She recognizes Blunt immediately, calls him by name, and lets him know that she remembers what his clergyman father did for a living. But of what else is this subtle, accomplished woman thinking? The question occurs to Blunt, even though he cannot risk asking it. It also occurred to Richard Hornby, reviewer of the play for the *Hudson Review.* Content to leave the question unanswered, Hornby nevertheless notes its effect on the flatfooted Blunt: "Bennett makes the Queen marvelously ambiguous; one never knows whether she is being naively comic or making shrewd double entendres."[3] An elegant conversationalist who never says more than she intends, HMQ keeps making Blunt fidget and squirm. She faults him on an observation he makes about art forgery, a topic that falls within his field of expertise. Wasting few social graces on him, she will not laugh at his jokes. And she throws him "a sharp look" (*SS* 50) when she believes him guilty of overstepping the bounds of propriety. She also voices a dislike for gossip (*SS* 48), a rhetorical mode on which espionage thrives, along with hearsay and rumor.

She tells Blunt, who has been feigning loyalty to her, that she finds forgery "fascinating" (*SS* 49). And then she says of a specific Old Master, "This can't be a forgery, it's in such and such a collection, its background and pedigree are impeccable—

besides, it has been vetted by the experts. . . . Isn't that how the argument goes" (*SS* 50)? If this clever, articulate woman is only discussing painting, Blunt is safe. But her remarks also apply both to him and to the security check that was run on him prior to his joining British Intelligence. And Blunt knows it, which is why he wipes his hands on a handkerchief he takes "nervously" from a pocket (*SS* 50). She keeps him within her snare. When he asks if something that belies its name deserves to be called an enigma, she replies, "That, I think, is the sophisticated answer" (*SS* 50). She is implying that this answer is not one she would give herself. And why should she? Having nothing to hide, she can afford frankness. On the other hand, his Byzantine indirection, fascinating as it is, amounts to nothing more than a cover-up. The lesson is clear. As in Henry James, sophistication in *Question* pales before simplicity, especially in cases where simplicity stands on a bedrock of honesty.

Bennett played the Blunt role in the first London production of *Question*. Intriguingly, he shows Blunt less sympathy than Burgess, Blunt's counterpart in the 1988 double bill staged as *Single Spies*. So addicted is Blunt to the casuistry that spying thrives on that the simple and the direct keep stumping him. When asked why he became a communist agent, the best answer he can muster is that "it seemed the right thing to do at the time" (*SS* 32). Yet this lame answer sounds worse coming from him than from Burgess, who replied with the same words to Coral Browne's question in *Englishman* (*SS* 10). Though both traitors know that the USSR never deserved their efforts, Burgess invested more of himself in what some view as the last great social cause of the twentieth century. He knew firsthand the squalor and the deceit infecting everyday life in the USSR; as has been seen, when challenged to cite a virtue of Soviet communism, he can only mention "the system" (*SS* 9). Yet five hard years in Moscow have earned him his evasion. Blunt, though, is cushioned by layers of prestige and luxury that Burgess, in his Moscow hovel, will never know.

And neither will Blunt, if Chubb has any say. Blunt cannot escape Chubb, whose reappearances on stage in Blunt's company suggest the imminence of the traitor's arrest. That traitor cannot resist him any more than he can going to jail. Advisedly, Chubb's first onstage appearance coincides with Blunt's words about both a martyred saint and Judas, two roles Blunt could imagine himself playing (*SS* 31). Chubb is next seen questioning him about the third man, the agent who helped Burgess and Maclean flee England under the noses of the Special Branch (*SS* 38). Chubb's questions here are pointed, even relentless. Yet Blunt, though perhaps evasive, neither loses patience with Chubb nor tries to dismiss him. The audience wonders why Chubb has such easy access to Blunt. Another mystery is the source of his power. Is he what's called in the spy trade Blunt's handler or controller?

He acts as if he is debriefing Blunt, asking him to identify the young men (his Cantab contemporaries?) whose images appear in the tray of slides he forces Blunt to look at. These youths may be suspected of having joined the Communist Party as students. But were he a Soviet agent himself, Chubb would already have a membership list. It is more likely that he is a British spy. He does talk about offering Blunt immunity (but not anonymity), perhaps in exchange for turning state's evidence. At the end, though, Chubb hints that his power to protect Blunt is waning: "You will be the object of scrutiny, explanations sought after, your history gone into. You will be named. Attributed" (*SS* 54). Then Chubb implies that, were Blunt to name his KGB source in England, the Special Branch might be persuaded to lengthen his leash. But Blunt starts talking about the famous art critic and collector Bernard Berenson. Blunt is going to jail. In a rough parallel with both Ibsen's Karsten Bernick of *The Pillars of Society* and Williams's Blanche Dubois, though, his downfall has coincided with his triumph. He will not betray his treachery. He protects his KGB contact, moreover, while wearing the full evening dress he had put on to give a speech at the Royal Academy Dinner. And he looks splendid.

His ability to hold a style has become a final refuge for this traitor. Once again, though, sophistication has lost out to common sense. Bennett takes some pains to portray Chubb as a suburban drone several cuts below Blunt socially. In the bourgeois mode, Chubb spends time looking at great art without being moved. He talks about his wife. Greeting the resplendent Blunt at the end of the play, Chubb insists that he would feel lost and displaced at a function as grand as the Royal Academy Dinner. Besides lacking the social credentials and the manner to merit an invitation, he does not have the wardrobe. Yet he has been studying art history in order to gain insight into Blunt, and, prosaic as it is, he introduces a slant on Michelangelo that surprises Blunt. Perhaps Blunt has underrated the English bourgeoisie. Chubb's gift for nuance, indirection, and thoroughness as a debriefer compels Blunt's full attention.

In 1990, Hornby called *Question* "the perfect play for its time, in a country struggling to redefine the nature of government and of art, and the relationship between them."[4] Hornby is right. *Question* makes most other spy dramas look clumsy and mean spirited. Bennett's 1988 one-acter has found the common truth in the myth of spying and has done so simply and elegantly by looking it straight in the eye.

IV

Hilary, the main figure of the full-length play *The Old Country,* resembles Guy Burgess of *An Englishman Abroad* in being an ex–Foreign Service chief who betrayed Britain and then defected to the USSR. But unlike both Burgess and the Blunt of *Question,* Hilary is a fictional character. He is also straight rather than gay, and he has a wife, Bron; no single spy, he. Bron flew to Moscow with him fourteen years before the continuous action described in Bennett's 1977 stage play, and she has stayed with him. Hilary also has a sister named Veronica. Veronica's husband, a fifty-six-year-old power broker named Duff adds tones of his own to the minisociety of the play. Duff once had a one-night stand with Eric, a young Englishman who later came to the USSR as part of a spy swap in which his wife Olga was a principal.

Olga is the only one of the play's six figures who is standing on native ground. But she does not stand very comfortably. She is Jewish in a country notorious for its anti-Semitism. Whether or not she muffed her assignment, she has to live under the cloud of having been caught by British Intelligence agents while spying for the Soviets in the UK. She feels uneasy in the presence of Hilary, who clearly dislikes her. Finally, she knows that her homesick younger husband Eric would leave her in a heartbeat if given the chance to return to England.

This ingrown society of cranky, displaced people lacks both focus and direction. The action these unfortunates help develop takes place in a country cottage too primitive to qualify as a dacha or even a bungalow. It is more of a lean-to or a shack. And its inhabitants, Hilary and Bron, are just as worn and weary as their summer digs. The revelation halfway into the first act that the two are in the USSR lends new and bitter meaning to some of their earlier comments, many of which deal with London institutions and landmarks. "Despite their exile, Hilary and Bron are more English than those who stayed behind," said Gilbert Cant in his *Time* review of the play. Cant adds, "she shuffles around in hearty tweeds, he frets over the decline of Lyons Teahouses."[5] Traitors in Bennett are ruled by the nostalgia and insularity Cant cites. Because Hilary has, in Bron, a permanent sympathetic audience, he vents his Englishness more than his fellow traitors Burgess and Blunt. Yet all three men long for a bygone Englishness, when everyday life was more decent and humane; when the Tories were benevolent; and when Londoners could find a Lyons within walking distance of job and home to serve them a good cup of tea. Champions of the ordinary, these men savor the familiar, the comfortable, and the recurrent as they existed, or were believed to have existed, a generation earlier.

The subject of betrayal preoccupies Hilary. And, like Burgess and Blunt, he tries to ease the guilt caused by his treason by indulging his bent for charm, irony, and nostalgia. His diversionary tactics sometimes fail him. Hilary is bored. Taking out a pistol when he spots strangers on his property discloses his hunger for decisive action. Another sign of his malaise is the dream he recounts in his second speech of the play. He tells about being alone one night in his childhood home when he thought that the home was being burgled. Though frightened, he took steps to protect his family. But when he was about to bring down a hammer on the head of one of the burglars, he recognized his intended victim as his father. That father, like many others in Bennett, is now infirm and institutionalized. Yet even if he is a secret sinner, he still represents the languishing fatherland Hilary betrayed and still loves.

Called by Bennett in *Writing Home* "an embittered, ironic figure" (*WH* 209), Hilary fled England after years of spying for the Kremlin when he thought that British intelligence agents were about to arrest him. Like Burgess in *Englishman,* he finds that traitors are universally despised. He got no warm welcome from his new hosts when he arrived in Moscow; nor has he been pampered during his long exile, even though he has become, in this interim, a Soviet citizen. Perhaps the dreariness of the past fourteen years has not surprised him or offended his sense of justice. His sister, Veronica, who has known him longer than any of the other characters in the play, says that he was always his worst enemy.[6] His self-divisions do run deep. Charming and witty as he is, he knows that his treachery caused the deaths of hundreds of his countrymen (the number thirty, evocative of Judas, is mentioned in the play's early moments [*OC* 10]). This carnage cannot be excused or laughed away. And if he tries to bury it in the glitter of social chic, the others will not let him. Recalling Coral Browne's rebuke to Burgess ("you pissed in our soup and we drank it" [*SS* 10]), Veronica tells him, "when you've . . .

about redemption through sex, but not in the way Geoffrey intended. The monogamous, monotheistic Christian-Western value system has let her down. What buoys her up is an adulterous tie with a twenty-six-year-old Hindu.

No catharsis crowns *Lentils.* All of Susan's cherished values have collapsed, and she has not found another set to replace them. By breaking the laws on which both her society and her husband's ministry rest, this alcoholic and adulteress reaps wide-scale gains, including Geoffrey's promotion to archdeacon. Rather than hiding Susan's drinking problem, Geoffrey goes public with it, proclaiming to his parishioners, in the nonjudgmental spirit of the 1980s, that she has joined Alcoholics Anonymous. And Susan directs the whole process, even though she does not understand why. A decade earlier, her drinking would have made her an object of scorn. But she remains silent in her puzzlement. Happily, she realizes that she embodies a truth she can only sabotage by exposing it to analysis or discussion now that Ramesh has left Leeds. If she has to keep quiet about the core reality of her recent life, her secrecy has gained her a comfort and a prestige beyond any enjoyed by Graham of *Chip,* who sacrificed more than Susan for the sake of reshaping the status quo.

Both narrators, though, owe whatever social identity they have to discretion. Irene Ruddock, the narrator of *A Lady of Letters,* offers another lesson on the same subject. Speaking out costs Miss Ruddock everything. To assert her importance, this lonely spinster inflates any quirk or eccentricity she perceives in others into a moral failing that must be reported straightaway to the local police or even to her representative in Parliament. Her opening words regarding a recent funeral, "I can't say the service was up to scratch" (44), lead to her disclosure that she wrote a complaining letter to the director of the crematorium where the funeral was held. And she had grounds for complaint; hearse drivers who smoke in view of the mourners *do* mar the dignity of a funeral service. Her complaints about the prison system also have merit. And if she overreacts to what she reads about English jails, at least she is not apathetic. Her letter to her member of Parliament reflects a courage and a commitment most people would be too lazy to muster in response to a civic issue. But her reformer's zeal knows no bounds. As in the case of her neighbors with the dying child, she demonizes people without first gathering supporting evidence. This arrogance has made her the worst kind of public nuisance—the one who always believes herself in the right. Because she knows more than her doctor, she stops using the medicine he has prescribed for her. In fact, she shows her contempt for him by flushing the medicine down the toilet.

A law unto herself, this atheist publicizes the alleged misdeeds of her neighbors and a local policeman (she has already told a pharmacist that his wife was a prostitute). She belongs in jail. What nobody could have predicted was how well she fares behind bars. Like Susan of *Lentils,* she finds that compounding her sins redeems both them and her. Just as Susan's adultery helps wean her from booze, Miss Ruddock's prison diary provides her an ideal outlet for her passion to write: "the other girls can't think what to put in theirs, me I can't think what to leave out," she says of this acceptable new outlet for her fabrications (*TH* 51). Though she is beyond change, her jail sentence shows her to be redeemable. She studies bookbinding, dressmaking, and typing, and she enjoys listening in on her fellow prisoners' discussions of sex. These discussions help her, too, since, through them, she learns about the thrills of sex, even though she may never savor them directly. Like Susan, she is a Thoreauvian heroine indirectly rewarded for violating some of society's strictest taboos. Changes occur in her immediately. Less brittle than before, she takes up both smoking and profanity. She even finds an outlet for her meddling in the behavior of her cell mate. After Bridget awakens from a dream about the child she killed, Miss Ruddock gets out of bed and holds her hand. That is all she does. There is no need to censure Bridget. She has already been punished. What is left is to comfort her, a small duty Miss Ruddock performs in keeping with her burgeoning humanity. Her physical confinement has created paths for her soul to expand into without her knowing why.

Bennett's next narrator, Lesley of *Her Big Chance,* is also swept along by currents she can neither understand nor control. Her opening words seize us: "I shot a man last week," she says, adding, "Still, I'm not going to get depressed about it." Seconds later, she heightens the dramatic tension by saying, "It was with a harpoon gun actually, but it definitely wasn't an accident" (*TH* 56). Ironically, this supposed desperado turns out to be one of the most passive, predictable narrators in the *Talking Heads* series. When she can find work, this actress (the only head with a job) appears in movies as a bit player. Yet even though she takes mostly nonspeaking roles, she feels that her talent will soon capture a film executive's attention and earn her star billing. Lesley has committed herself totally to the art of acting. Perhaps Bennett was thinking of this high-mindedness when he enigmatically called her "wholly modern (while being quite old-fashioned)" (*TH* 8–9). Alert to Stanislavskian matters like dramatic motivation and psychological consistency, she keeps making suggestions to a newly met director who is thinking about casting her in a film. The prospect of playing the role of a character named Travis excites her, and she wants to lend the role as much weight as she can. But those in charge of making the film are more interested in her thirty-eight-inch bust than in her ideas. In fact, ideas would encumber her role, which demands that she appear naked twice on-screen and say only the name of her victim, Alfredo, before harpooning him.

The harpooning scene is shot in just one take, which attests to the shoddiness of the film, which will be released on video-tape only in West Germany and perhaps Turkey. Lesley's big chance isn't that big, after all. But she must pretend it is. Like Arthur Miller's salesman, she cannot let her spirits drop. And she tries hard to keep them high. Some of the things she says to win people's respect diminish her. Citing the arrangements that Roman Polanski provided his actors during the shooting of *Tess* (1979), like croissants, hair dryers, and immaculate field toilets, she complains that the facilities on the set of the video in which she is acting fall below her usual working standard. The answer she gets, "Let's face it, dear. You're not used to working," silences her (*TH* 61). As much as she denies it, she is lucky to be acting in a low-distribution soft-porn video movie. A misunderstanding won her the part of Travis in the first place, since the film's producers were looking for a fluent speaker of French who could also water-ski. A further regret comes in her discovery that the person coaching her during one of the sequences is not the director but only a midlevel functionary.

But any pain caused by this regret she keeps to herself. She also glosses over the fact that she sleeps with men to get auditions and acting roles (in the course of *Chance,* she has four bedmates, all one-night stands). She is speaking more accurately than she knows or admits when she says in the last line of her monologue, "Acting is really just giving" (*TH* 67). And her sexual appeal, if not her sexual readiness, *has* won her the small success she enjoys. An annoyance on the set, she challenges the judgment of the production crew; she brings her own unauthorized props onto the shooting stage; her gauche response to a joke both spoils the joke and peeves its teller. Yet undeterred, she keeps trying to dignify her small part. Nor does she relent in her perception of her career as an adventure, a means of self-fulfillment, and a source of camaraderie. Thus she is shocked and hurt when both the crew and the talent of her film-in-progress go off to dinner without asking her to join them. She is always being slighted. But when she tries to bid farewell to the other members of her unit after the shoot is finished and finds them already gone, the stab of pain she feels boosts her standing with us.

These others see acting as only a job. Now that the shoot along the marina is over, they are ready to move on. Despite her gaffes and misjudgments, Lesley invested the shoot with humanity. She thought more about it than her counterparts, risked more for it, and put more energy into it. Much of her dedication is bogus. She removes her bikini on a wintry shooting set in the name of professionalism. She also convinces herself that she is

behaving professionally by sleeping with anyone who can further her career. But at least she has found a calling that is worth
sacrificing her dignity to. Already in her thirties, she has been
making sacrifices for some time. Her belief that a brilliant acting career awaits her is a piece of arrant self-deception. Yet the
strength of her belief denotes a courage that deserves our approval. Bennett must have been thinking of her when he said of
his seven talking heads, "They are somewhat black, but there is
also some sense of redemption or triumph in them."[6]

Lesley's senior by some twenty-five years, Muriel Carpenter of *Soldiering On* is also threatened more by blackness.
Sheridan Morley emphasized the grimness of her prospects in
his *Spectator* review of the June 1996 London stage revival of
Talking Heads. Morley calls Muriel, "a newly widowed house-
wife . . . who in the immediate aftermath of her husband's death
is robbed by their beloved son and brought up against the still
more awful reality that the cause of their daughter's mental illness is that she was sexually abused by her own father."[7]

Muriel's fortunes run counter to those of Susan in *Lentils*.
Depressed at the outset, Susan moved from gloom to sunshine
even if the sunshine made her blink. Muriel, on the other hand,
comes before the audience as "a brisk, sensible woman in her
late fifties" who lives in "a comfortable home" (*TH* 70). Probably the most educated talking head, she also has both the inner
resources and the financial security to look forward to a couple
of decades of serenity. But, as Morley suggested, her
misperception of her children costs her everything.

For one thing, her overweight son Giles (who recalls the fat
schemer Prin of *Madness*) always fought with his father. Per-

haps he convinced himself that surviving the ordeal of being Ralph's son has entitled him to his father's money even though that father disinherited him. Perhaps he is punishing Muriel for having allowed Ralph to molest Margaret. Claiming to be protecting Muriel, Giles convinces her that, even though well off, she has a "liquidity problem" that dictates the sale of some of her assets (*TH* 73). Then, supposedly helping her avoid estate taxes, he carts away some of her more expensive household items, like pictures and clocks. Before long, he has gotten her to "sign lots of papers" as well, allegedly to secure her home (*TH* 73). But she loses the home. She is last seen settling into a boarding-house as a result of Giles's having squandered, embezzled, and lost her and Ralph's life savings. Her downfall has leached her spirits. Presumably comfortable throughout most of her adult life, Muriel now complains about the price of morning coffee (*TH* 78). And Giles will not buy her a cup, either. He and his wife haven't visited for more than a month, a real blow to Muriel because she has lost access to her beloved grandchildren.

Yet she would rather pine over this loss than ponder the possibility that Giles stole her money. Once she admits this possibility, she will have to question his motives. And any guilt that attaches to her stems from her having failed to protect Margaret from Ralph. Her guilt runs higher than she admits. After the sale of the Carpenter home, Margaret is placed in a mental hospital, and not an elegant one: the beds in her ward are jammed together; there is only one toilet on her floor; she has to walk outside to reach the hospital's cafeteria. Her presence in the ward mystifies her mother. Though Muriel has accepted Margaret's mental illness, she denies its cause. "Why have we been singled out?" she protests. "Loving parents. Perfectly normal childhood, then this" (*TH* 75).

But she drops the odd hint that Margaret's childhood was not normal because Ralph bestowed the wrong kind of love on her. "Ralph and Giles never got on . . . whereas, it's funny, he was always dotty about Mags" (*TH* 73), Muriel recalls just before discussing Giles's supposed attempt to improve her cash flow. Then she refers to Mags as "Daddy's little girl," calling particular attention to "those great legs" (*TH* 74). The term *great legs* is not one most mothers would use in connection with their daughters. But it could have come from a father who found his daughter sexually exciting. What could have also come from Ralph was guilt, which would explain why he took greater care protecting Margaret in his will than he did Muriel (*TH* 78), whom he might have been punishing for conniving in his disgrace. Like *Chip in the Sugar* before it, *Soldiering On* deals with a family drama that grows uglier and uglier as more evidence comes from its beleaguered narrator.

Doris, the talking head of *A Cream Cracker under the Settee,* is an older working-class foil of Muriel. Barred from doing housework, this seventy-five-year-old who uses a pacemaker and suffers from dizzy spells nevertheless emboldens herself to dust the wedding photo overlooked by the cleaning woman sent by the council. Whereas Muriel denies the existence of dirt, Doris attacks it. Demonstrating that most of the issues raised by Bennett have at least two sides, Doris would not have had to clean up after Zulema if Zulema had done her job properly. But Doris disapproved of the way her now-dead husband cleaned house, too. Perhaps she is as carping and censorious as Bennett's letter-

writing Irene Ruddock. Doris's first words, "It's such a silly thing to have done" and "I should never have tried to dust," convey her annoyance with herself (*TH* 82). She has already been punished for overstepping. She fell and dropped the wedding photo she was dusting, and it now lies on the floor with a crack running across it. Having lost the use of her legs as a result of her fall, she has slumped to the floor. She refuses the help of a passing policeman even though, hunkered near her front door, she cannot move. Perhaps she is too embarrassed to be seen sitting in her excreta. But staving off embarrassment is not a goal worth dying for. Guilt kept Muriel Carpenter from defending herself against her son. It is curious that Doris rejects her chance to prolong her existence, meager as it is. She may be punishing herself for some misdeed.

In his introduction, Bennett cites Doris's "determination to dust" (*TH* 8) as both *her* downfall and that of her husband. A likeness between herself and Wilfred (which is also the name of the child-molesting father in *Enjoy*) has established itself in her distressed mind. "Cracked the photo. We're cracked, Wilfred," she declaims while looking at the broken picture frame (*TH* 83). The frame also evokes her newborn son who died decades earlier, so misshapen that the midwife dissuaded Doris from naming him. If there is a link between this calamity and Doris's passion for cleanliness, it is not spelled out. But it is perhaps alluded to. A forgotten cream cracker has slid under the settee against which Doris is spread-eagled. Had she not been perched in her unlikely spot, she would have missed it. Obviously, Zulema never saw it either or she would have disposed of it. Its presence gladdens Doris, vindicating her belief that she was justified in cleaning up after Zulema. Then her monologue does the same kind of about-face that occurred at the end of *Lentils* and *Letters.* Doris eats the dusty cracker.

In what may be her last living act, either she is celebrating her triumph over the slipshod Zulemas of the world or she has finally intuited both the harmlessness and the ubiquity of dust. Insofar as nature abhors a vacuum, dust coats everything, including food. Eating the dusty cracker may even have added some minutes to Doris's life. But she lacks the wit to admit this possibility. Committed to habits of mind long in place, this kindly provincial elder remains trapped in the same current that swept away her husband and perhaps her baby boy. Like Muriel of *Soldiering On,* Doris suffers her worst hardships late in life. And she has no offspring to lighten her burden because she filled herself with so many antitoxins during her pregnancy that she stifled her son's development. But for Bennett, the story of her warped purity would have gone unheard. Saying what he does about her, he shows that this silence would have been both a pity and an injustice, even to his audiences. In some contexts, dirt can work better than cleanliness. Bennett has performed a humane service by focusing on the Dorises in our midst and illuminating the processes that make them such proud, pathetic figures.

II

Thora Hird, the original Doris figure in *Cream Cracker,* appears as a dying man's sister in *Intensive Care* (1982), a Bennett telescript that includes still another talking head, Bennett himself, who plays dying Frank Midgley's son, Denis, "a shy school-

teacher" (*WH* 121) of thirty-nine. *Care* brings back other familiar elements from the Bennett canon. Like Gilbert Chilvers of *A
Private Function,* Denis has a sexually frustrated and resentful
wife named Joyce who looks after her elderly mother. But the
mother is not threatened by death. A skewed mirror image of
Cream Cracker's Doris, Frank Midgley collapses at home with
a stroke and is not found for two days, during which time he
contracts hypothermia and pneumonia, which will soon kill him.

Like that other dying father, Joey Wyman of *Rolling Home,*
Frank attracts three generations of relatives to his sick room.
Besides his sister Kitty (who's played by Thora Hird), there's
his brother Ernest, *his* married son Hartley, daughter-in-law, Jean,
and their children. Owing to the stress of watching a close relative die, family antagonisms flare out as they did in *Rolling Home,*
with Jean carping, perhaps with some justification, about Ernest's
stinginess with money. Though Ernest mentions some foreign
trips he is looking forward to taking, he tells his comatose brother,
"We can't go on like this, you know. I can't run to the fares" (*OA*
195). But matching such resentments are the odd jokes and moments of tenderness and fun that pierce the gloom. Rounding
out Bennett's picture of hospital routine are the various doctors
and nurses, some coldly efficient but others sympathetic not only
to Frank's circle but also to his fellow patients and their weary,
anxious relatives, who are standing by in the intensive care unit's
waiting room, where talk ranges from outgoing telephone reports on the condition of different patients to discussions of the
usefulness of the unit's resuscitating machines.

The script's main character, Denis Midgley, appears twice
at a kitchen table with a carving knife nearby (*OA* 172, 177).
Called "a pill" (*OA* 180) by his wife, Joyce, tentative, cautious

Midgley would like to be more daring and reckless. Thus the knife with which he is associated is an ironic symbol. Perhaps he is even too detached to be a good teacher. When the mother of one of his students explains that the student's menstrual problems are distracting her from her studies, Midgley talks about Coretta's poor attention span and "her poor performance in Use of English" (*OA* 173). He is awkward around others. Another parent accuses him of having failed to teach proper speech, and two hospital officials scold him for lying down in the waiting room and for tracking mud into the ICU.

These reproofs upset Midgley, who feels that his wife and father both despise him. The hopeless wreck of a father, usually a reprobate in Bennett, gains new stature in *Care*. Always a reproach to Midgley, Frank takes on an intimidating new vibrancy on his deathbed. Everybody admired Frank, Midgley learns. His sister Kitty calls him "a saint" (*OA* 182), recalling how much he enjoyed helping others with menial chores like shoveling snow. After the death of his wife—an unpleasant woman whom Midgley is said to take after (*OA* 180, 182)—Frank won the heart of a rich socialite whose marriage proposal he rejected because he did not want to feel beholden. And now this paragon who stood between Midgley and manhood is dying without Midgley having to raise a finger. But even this stroke of fortune rankles the son. Perhaps had he raised a finger, Frank might be his normal self. Having skipped his usual weekend visit to his father, Midgley lost the chance to bring Frank to the hospital before he became comatose: "I'm sorry Dad" (*OA* 181) is one of the first things he tells an unhearing Frank after entering his room. And now his guilt is given a painful new wrench when he hears the night nurse speculate about Frank's bygone sexual charms while washing the dying man's thighs.

Midgley is so shaken that, while sleeping in his van in the hospital's parking lot, he dreams that his father has climbed into the van with him and driven it away. Then the painful sexual motif that had erupted in the hospital takes new life. Midgley's dead mother, now a young woman, enters the van, and Frank puts his hand on her knee. The next dream sequence shows a grimy Frank running down a huge slag heap and across a field, where he joins Midgley, now a child, and his mother. Midgley had just told his mother, "It's a lovely field. We can sit here all day. Just the two of us" (*OA* 205). But the twosome soon becomes a trio with Midgley pushed to the sidelines. Jarred into wakefulness, he vows not to yield any more ground in the one-sided Oedipal struggle. He wants to prove, to himself mostly, that his filial love can overcome his jealousy. And his proof will take the form of being at Frank's bedside at the moment of death. He has to atone for having skipped his regular weekend visit. Despite being sent home by a matron, a doctor, and his Uncle Ernest, he stays in the hospital complex. But something besides filial love is motivating him. He senses that Frank "wants me to let him down" to prove his moral superiority over his son (*OA* 208).

The complex of emotions battering Midgley makes this tame, predictable homebody act with uncharacteristic wildness. Without premeditation, he asks the kindly, helpful night nurse in the ICU to have sex with him. And surprisingly, his request is granted. "Hold on, Dad, hold on," Midgley tells an unconscious Frank as he goes off to bed Valery (*OA* 203). The psychic energies swirling around the sickroom have aligned themselves in Midgley's favor. Though hearing Valery musing about Frank's sexuality wounded Midgley, the experience also roused his lust. And now that lust is about to be sated. Vitality is abroad. Frank's lungs and heart have shown so much improvement that he is being moved from the ICU. But these signs of hope are false. Frank dies unexpectedly while Midgley is having sex with Valery in her room. Frank may well have withdrawn his will to live when he learned that Midgley had left his bedside. At any rate, he died with a smile after asking for Midgley. He may have deliberately sent his son a false signal of hope in order to score one last point. Frank's death drains Midgley's sexual romp with Valery of warmth and promise. It also costs him whatever self-esteem he had hoped to recoup by staying at his post.

The knowledge that he had succeeded in his scheme to crush Midgley's spirits might have helped Frank die happily. Perhaps he and Joyce got along so well because, in Midgley, they had a common enemy. The end of the teleplay shows that enemy depressed and alone, walking down a dreary institutional corridor in the school where he teaches. Then the camera jump cuts to another long, sterile corridor at the hospital where Frank died. Midgley has just scolded his son Colin for kissing his girlfriend within hours of Frank's death. Most people with less education than Midgley would have spotted his hypocrisy. But they would have also appreciated the psychological context of his hypocritical reproach. His father is dead, and his wife, who despises him, has undermined his authority over his son by sanctioning Colin's kissing of his girlfriend. Midgley feels cut off from his family. Perhaps he belongs in the cold, gray corridor where he is last seen.

Like most of the other scripts Bennett set in the industrial North of England, *Me, I'm Afraid of Virginia Woolf* evokes the urban realism of working-class films like Jack Clayton's *Room at the Top* (1959) and Bryan Forbes's *L-Shaped Room* (1963). Other trademark characteristics of Bennett's teledramas come into view. Actress Thora Hird, who played both Kitty in *Intensive Care* and Doris in *Cream Cracker,* returns to *Me* as another Doris, the anxious widowed mother of the play's main figure, Trevor Hopkins. Even though Hopkins, like Denis Midgley, teaches English, he is not played by Bennett. Bennett enters the action only as a voice or voice-over. He acts the role of narrator, an important, if understated, presence. This importance can be gauged by the economy he brings to the play's structure. By supplying background information, providing interscenic summaries, and pointing out the difference between what Hopkins says and what he means, this choric figure helps Bennett cover a great deal of thematic ground in his hour-long script.

The easily cowed Hopkins would apologize for his existence if he could. "With you it's too much sorry," an acquaintance says rightly of this liar and hypochondriac who would rather follow the rules than his instincts (*WD* 62). The thirty-five-year-old Hopkins has a secure job doing something he enjoys at decent pay. But his eagerness to avoid offending others has made him acutely anxious. The script's first scene shows him performing a characteristic gesture. Entering a doctor's waiting room, he takes the only available seat, next to a young woman. Some minutes later, he notices that all the other seats in the room are empty. He wonders if he should move to one of them. Staying put, he fears, runs the risk of appearing forward, even though his nose is buried in a book. But by moving, he could insult his neighbor. His book, which he always carries to spare him the disapproving or threatening looks of others, cannot fend off the trouble his hypersensitivity keeps inviting. Because names confer identity, his hatred of his first name implies a self-hatred borne out by his acts. Irresolute, dependent, and devious, this lecturer at a polytechnic in Halifax has some of the worst faults ascribed to academics. His students seem to hold him in contempt. After coming to his sparsely attended class ten minutes late, he sees that the pictures of E. M. Forster and Virginia Woolf he chose as visual aids have been adorned with a beard, mustache, and huge breasts.

Dave Skinner, Hopkins's brightest student and the play's spokesman for working-class vigor (his front name is the same as that of D. H. Lawrence), notes his teacher's preference for writers of great technical skill whose blood runs thin. Skinner has hit on something important. (He "wasn't exactly Clint Eastwood," Skinner says of Forster [*WD* 52].) It is suitable that the one lecture Hopkins gives during the play deals with two writers who shunned the rough and the raw in favor of charting the fluctuations of their characters' sensibilities. Hopkins's attraction to what some have called the limp-wristed school of English writing squares with his reticence, timidity, and fear of provincial uncouthness, qualities he has been using his education to transcend.

To escape the influence of his mother, Hopkins has been dating a yoga teacher named Wendy. It is consistent with his self-loathing, though, that in Wendy he has chosen a woman he clashes with. She is as aggressively confrontational as he is evasive and anxious. Her passion for the free, the natural, and the spontaneous overwhelms him. Thus he slips out of her bedroom, where he had gone to spend the night, troubled by her talk on subjects like the benefits of making love with the lights on and the regrets she harbors over never having seen her father naked. This enthusiast's words to her students catch the pitch and the tone of the new mind-body harmony Hopkins finds so grating: "Let your skeleton grow heavy but your body light. Take the left side of your face to the left. Take the right side of your face to the right. Take the back of your head to the front of your head. And, in your own time . . . let the silence in. Let your eyes become heavy. Slowly open your eyes and let the peace in" (*WD* 55). As so often happens with probers of their cosmic energy, Wendy mismanages the basics. She gets her muesli and yogurt all over her blouse, chin, and hair, and, while rebuking Hopkins for eating fried food, she spills her own dinner on the floor. If, as she claims, the body is "the basic syntax in the grammar of humanism" (*WD* 67), her own physical welfare suffers from an overdose of the linguistic pap she has substituted for solid nourishment.

A better match for Hopkins, though he would be shocked to admit it to himself, is the twenty-five-year-old married father, Bill Skinner. His interest in Skinner shatters Hopkins's defenses. He responds to Skinner's invitation to have a drink by asking him if he is married. Then he flusters; he immediately regrets asking the question lest Skinner think it an indirect accusation that he is gay. Poised and unrushed, Bennett tones in the human background rather than segueing to matters of plot and structure. Before approaching any kind of understanding with Skinner, Hopkins faces two ordeals. Still feeling emotionally drained by Wendy's candor, he sees on the bus a devouringly amorous couple he cannot ignore, much as he tries. He is accused of voyeurism and punched in the face by his hot-blooded lout of an accuser. The bus conductor advises him to go to the infirmary, which, standing beyond the district where Hopkins lives, costs him another five pence to reach.

Then, in the play's only structural flaw, coincidence materializes Bill Skinner. The two men go together to the outpatient clinic, where the blood dripping from Hopkins's nose mars his copy of a Virginia Woolf novel. Truth has come to Hopkins in violence, not in fact. The shrinking soul who had been teaching bloodless books to his students has received the infusion of iron and sinew he needs. The lesson helps him. It took a fist in the face to show him his homosexuality. The "wicked" (*WD* 71) smile he directs at Skinner shows that, unlike the old Hopkins, this new man will seize the chance to renew himself. In an audacious piece of cinematic shorthand, Bennett makes the point by catching Skinner and the leering Hopkins in a freeze frame for the rolling of the credits while the music from *South Pacific*'s "I'm in Love with a Wonderful Guy" fills the sound track.

Bloodshed and embarrassment have created the hope of redemption through love. But the script's ending is, at most, guardedly optimistic. Having a lover will discommode Skinner, inasmuch as he comes to Hopkins laden with family duties. Hopkins's own self-imposed burdens could easily smother any budding romantic tie with Skinner before the tie develops. Brittle and defensive, Hopkins has, until the play's last scene, kept all the other characters at bay. But perhaps Bennett does not want to pair him off with Skinner as much as put him on the path of self-acceptance. Though it may be months or even years before

Hopkins feels sexually comfortable with someone, he has at least learned where his best chances lie.

While inviting thoughts about Hopkins's future, Bennett also portrays the everydayness of the industrial North. One brilliant vignette describes a sardonic teacher of mechanical drawing at the polytechnic and his class of gusty, gleeful students mocking Hopkins's attempt to find the desecrater of his visual aids. The best scenes in *Me* do not advance the plot but, rather, convey the smug, flinty energy of English provincialism. These scenes may have also cost Bennett the most effort. He calls the "main scene" of *Me* the episode in which Hopkins's mother shows up at the polytechnic's cafeteria to question her son about his personal life over dinner (*WH* 274). Mrs. Hopkins is relentless in her criticisms of the cafeteria's food and toilet facilities as well as in her questions about both her son's job and his relationship with Wendy. She uses two different approaches to convey her disapproval of her son. Although it is clear that she is motivated by love, her implacability leaves Hopkins exhausted. Nicholas Wapshott's appreciation of Bennett, published in the *Times* a week before *Me* premiered on television, nonetheless details the strengths that distinguish this December 1978 work. Bennett's "keen powers of observation, his love of the north and its people, and his knowledge of himself" freed him to take risks in *Me* that can exhilarate and appall.[8] The work infuses vigor and abundance into a complex emotional tension. One of Bennett's more troubling teledramas, it is also one of his sharpest and most memorable.

The Old Crowd (January 1979) invites the same high praise. The corrosive humor and the racketing, jittery energy of this Lindsay Anderson collaboration qualify it as Bennett's most experimental work. Writing in *Sight and Sound,* John Russell Taylor called it "a sort of surrealistic farcical tragedy set among the crumbling ruins of the upper classes in a still unfurnished house about two hours from Horsham." Yet Taylor believes the made-for-television film to be "arid and sterile," calling its stage effects "stilted and self-conscious."[9] This attack was accompanied by others. In his introduction to *Crowd,* Anderson, who may have scripted part of the work in addition to directing it, quotes reviews from newspapers like the *Sunday Express,* the *Observer,* and the *Sunday Telegraph,* whose collective "barrage of outrage" against the work included terms like "Meaningless," "Tosh," and "Rubbish" (*WD* 169). *Crowd is* nightmarish, absurdist, and a little threatening, but it is also as socially relevant as it is socially disruptive. An attempt, says Anderson, to capture "the strain, menace, [and] disintegration of English life" (*WD* 163), it describes quantitative changes inducing qualitative ones.

A rich couple named George and Betty have decided to host a housewarming party for their friends (the old crowd) in their new Edwardian home even though their furniture has not yet arrived. The preponderance of wrongness in the action shows that lunacy has entrenched itself firmly in the characters' lives. First, the furniture has been missing for ten days despite needing only two hours to travel from its former location in Horsham to its projected target in north London. If it ever does arrive, it will face cheerless surroundings. A mirror is cracked, three of the house's four toilets are not usable, and a television set has stopped working. As if a virus of breakdown and collapse has poisoned everything, this ruin has infected the human realm.

The parents of one of the party guests have already died in two separate plane crashes. Another guest dies during the party, perhaps impelled to the grave by a slide-show image of a boy who exploded while walking on a land mine.

Signs of health and happiness are nonexistent. The lights are out on George and Betty's street, and the phone booth standing on the corner has been vandalized. In addition, huge potholes have been forming in the streets of towns in England, Scotland, and Wales. Nor can any signs be detected that the devastation will let up. Unemployment has become a huge problem. One guest tells about an electrical parts firm in the Midlands folding and putting 250 people out of work because a similar firm in Taiwan can sell the parts at a third of the price. The same guest explains how, on a bus, his cousin saw a youth who had concealed under his coat a severed human hand on which there was a ring he was trying to pry off. Perhaps he was rocking in distress from side to side, because the ring wouldn't budge. Perhaps his distress had darker sources. A colorless, awkward man who spends more time listening to his transistor radio than he does talking to the other party guests finds England baffling. "If we were in South America I could tell you exactly what to do," says Dickie when asked about the advisability of selling a forest in Sussex (*WD* 193).

The baffled Dickie is baffling himself. Perhaps the film's richest character, this financial wizard has, in Stella, a wife who deceives him in open view of anyone who cares to look. Stella's choice of a lover, the hired waiter Glyn, exemplifies the film's strategy of injecting the extraordinary into the mundane. Like several other leading motifs in *Crowd,* the union of Glyn and

Stella combines a surreal sense of the everyday with the coexistence of incompatibilities. In his twenties, Glyn displays at first a good deal of discomfort and insecurity (traits that he shares with Dickie and that thus endear him to Stella?). No sooner is he in George and Betty's house than he needs a toilet. Unfortunately, to get to the house's only working toilet, he has to walk through the room in which Betty is arranging herself for the evening. Her annoyance at being interrupted leaves him unfazed, though. Perhaps it even shows him that he need not worry about offending his betters. The ensuing behavior of this out-of-work actor shows the effects of his recognition. Particularly in a place as adrift as England in the late 1970s, life consists largely of dramatic performance, freeing a Glyn or a Stella to invent personalities for themselves as they please. They need not worry about stumbling over pieces of furniture as they pursue their goals. Life without furniture or guidelines gives free rein to the impulsiveness that makes self-invention so easy.

The blind piano tuner seen at the outset foreshadows the metaphorical groping that will characterize much of what follows. The impulses are always blind. Also, the action unfolds on a poorly lit street, and, as has been seen, one of the guests dies during a slide show, which presumably takes place in a darkened room. What is more, no relief will come from tradition. The erosion of authority takes different forms in *Crowd.* A couple comes to the door wearing headgear that makes them look like air-raid wardens. But they turn out to be the entertainers George and Betty have hired for the evening. Besides, the London Blitz took place forty years earlier. Air-raid wardens no longer exist—they would have no job to do. But the police still have a function. No helpful policeman has stationed himself on George and Betty's street, though, to direct the guests to their destination. Glyn presumably plays policemen's parts (*WD* 182) when he can find work as an actor. But as the married Stella's lover, he breaks the law rather than protecting it. A policeman does show himself, but on a slide, where he cannot help anybody. Finally, the piano tuner had to quit the police force when he lost his sight. So it's just as well that he leaves George and Betty's house before the guests arrive. He could not help them, anyway.

Glyn, the pretend policeman, needs no white stick. He goes straight to his object. In one of *Crowd*'s most mystical metaphors and bizarre mood shifts, he puts his hand "momentarily but purposely" on Stella's breast while taking her coat. Her response, "Oh, thank you very much," while showing Glyn that he has not offended her, ignores the question of whether he and she have already met (*WD* 189). Perhaps such formalities lack meaning in their milieu. In any case, Glyn feels encouraged. More encouragement follows. During the final stages of dinner, Stella drops her napkin "fairly obviously" with Glyn standing nearby (*WD* 203). He returns the napkin to her, but only after removing one of her shoes, pocketing it, and then, in perhaps the play's boldest stroke, cutting a hole in her stocking and sucking her big toe. Thus Stella becomes the fourth female in Bennett, following others in *Rolling Home, All Day on the Sands,* and *Enjoy,* who appears either on stage or on camera semishod. Being unbalanced or off kilter, though, has not chilled her lust. Hearing the song, "Because," whose popularity at weddings stems from its message of enduring, fully committed love, inspires her to sleep with Glyn. In line with the irreverent spirit of the play, an added dollop of incentive might have come from the truth that she and Glyn are strangers who may never see each other again. She hobbles upstairs, followed by Glyn, who also follows her into the nearest room. But the room isn't empty, as if they care. The couple recline together behind a television set being watched by the elderly mother of either Betty or George, a woman known only as the Old Lady.

Obviously Glyn enjoyed his romp with Stella. Tumbling the richest and perhaps most beautiful woman at he party has emboldened him. When next seen downstairs, he is light years away from the awkward, ill-clad servant seen earlier. He pees in the kitchen sink and, without washing his hands, cuts himself a slice of ham. Then, significantly, Totty joins the party. But she is not only the last of the invited guests to arrive. She has also come alone, and, say reports circulated among the others, she has only six months to live. But she will not live that long. This last guest to arrive will be the first to leave. Now the timing of her arrival has made her look like the product of the rut that just took place upstairs. Ominously, neither Glyn nor his fellow servant Harold helps her out of her coat. For, although she could have used some help, this monumental blue blood seems to be a possible savior in a "cockeyed world" (*WD* 186) that cries out for salvation. A virus that kills its victims two hours after infecting them, it is said, thrives on the drugs prescribed to kill it, turning the hospitals where the drugs are administered into killing fields.

Totty's words to George, "I can do anything. Anything I want. It's wonderful" (*WD* 210), suggest that she can halt this plague. But she has only come to say goodbye to her friends,

and she forgets her parting message to them. Her tragic farewell remains unspoken. As Ionesco did in *The Chairs* (1952), Bennett shows the impossibility of communicating one's private vision. Totty dies with heroic dignity, anyway. By holding a mirror to her face to find out whether she is breathing, a character invokes Lear's heart-wrenching attempt to find life in Cordelia. Then Totty's corpse is arranged to evoke Hamlet's as it is taken from the stage. But whatever tragic dignity Bennett imparts to Totty he soon undercuts. The glass held over her to check her breathing, unlike Lear's tidy hand mirror, is large and clumsy to handle. Also, the overhead shot of Totty being carried offstage includes parts of the studio beyond the confines of the shooting set, picking up some television monitors and various crew members. Totty's death is just a theatrical conceit, undeserving of our tears. Even her survivors are unmoved. In unison, they sing "Goodnight, Ladies," to show their lack of emotion. Then they bid George and Betty polite goodbyes, leaving their hosts to dispose of the corpse as they may.

This stridency is but one of many. As he did in *Our Winnie* and *Soldiering On,* Bennett tallies the cost of keeping up appearances, a motif in Bennett that Morley has discussed: "Better perhaps than any dramatist since Rattigan, Bennett captures the clenched loneliness at the center of English family life complete with all its evasions and hypocrisies and the deals done for the sake of a bit of peace and quiet to be achieved at no matter what emotional cost."[10] But Bennett has a more caustic visual imagination than Rattigan to match his more anarchic moral sensibility. Some of this subversiveness declares itself in his portrayal of the woman known only as the Old Lady. In a film featuring people of glamour and power, of cachet and cash, this discard remains on screen by herself at the end of both halves of the hour-long production. Like Grandma in Edward Albee's *American Dream* (1960), the Old Lady represents a set of bygone values the other characters have helped destroy. Nor would they listen if she told them how to resist the deathliness looming around them. She has accepted her obsolescence and perhaps even relishes it. Apropos of little being discussed at the time, a character says, out of her hearing, "These days you are on your own. Wartime" (*WD* 189). He is right. The film describes the war of all against all.

A toast proposed by George to "Absent friends" (*WD* 201) echoes the moment in Noël Coward's *Private Lives* from which it was taken. The echo is intentional because, like Coward's 1940 comedy, *Crowd* describes love as combat. A character frustrated in love like Pauline (played by Rachel Roberts) prefigures the destructive outcome of this conjunction by acting suicidal. Pauline's suicide might even amuse the Old Lady. The end of part 1 of *Crowd* shows her reveling in the death of some youngsters in a car crash depicted on her television. At the end of *Crowd*, though, she is not watching any program. Her television has stopped working. But it may start up again, she tells George, switching it back on after he turns it off. As George said earlier, "life goes on" (*WD* 204). And she wants to view the process from her eyrie, savoring every step in the collapse, an event that could easily occur before any of the guests assembled below attain her old age—their punishment for ignoring her.

Lindsay Anderson might have been thinking of disintegration and collapse when he said that he wanted to develop the epical qualities of Bennett's script. Like the bareness of the house in which the dinner party takes place, Betty and George's determination to host the party creates a drive that contrasts admirably with the bizarre events unfolding on the small screen. This relentlessness takes on both depth and mystery because of the camera's occasional tendency to track to other cameras and the technicians staffing them just off the set. These tracking shots give the film an improvised air. As production flaws, they also provide a sense of security. We are only watching a TV film, after all, one, moreover, whose integrity has been besmirched by camera gaffes. No need to worry that any of the distress portrayed on the screen could threaten *us*. Yet Anderson jostles us out of our security. He explains his "reality-juggling" as a protest against naturalistic video technique, which, in his opinion, endorses the status quo (*WD* 173). Scrambling and stylizing the production of *The Old Crowd* he commends as liberating, since the work was commissioned for television, "the most conformist of the media" (*WD* 161). The distortions and dissonances in *Crowd* provoke deep questions. For instance, though we are now watching a television film, we may soon be appearing in one that the Old Lady upstairs will chuckle over. And it will be no light domestic comedy of manners.

The technical crew and equipment that come into view while George and Betty start to waltz grandly break the continuity of mood that has been building. No groundswell of harmony and melody will soar to a happy finale. The possibility that the members of the production team who keep appearing on screen may be actors rather than technicians also gives the unsettling sense that *Crowd,* by wrenching viewer expectations, is putting us at risk. For if the technicians are acting out roles written into the script, then who is manning the cameras, lights, and sound system? Unless a capable technical staff is doing these vital jobs, the film will never be produced, and nobody will witness mankind's common story. Like Totty, we will all die without first communicating our vision of the meaning of our downfall. Bennett and Anderson have extended the menace and the fury they have portrayed as a farrago of jazzy rhythms, jump cuts, and conversations nearly Chekhovian in their tact and sobriety. Though panned by its reviewers, *Crowd* discloses in Bennett a stunning new gift for recording the world around him. He has written in *The Old Crowd* an abrasive extravaganza meant to challenge our complacency. His efforts show him taking on the burden and the imperative of the vanguard artist.

Marks, a work of domestic realism first shown on BBC-TV2 in December 1982, exerts a strong grip without being experimental. As was seen in the transition from *Forty Years On* to *Enjoy,* the closer a Bennett work moves to the industrial North, the fewer cosmopolitan touches it includes. The crucial factor is what is usually called chemistry. The inspiration Bennett gets from his home base of Yorkshire gives him the confidence to dispense with literary dazzle. Warmth replaces brilliance. The resonant title, *Marks,* alludes to John Locke's notion of the tabula rasa: everybody resembles a blank slate or page at birth, and our experiences mark us in ways that create our unique selfhoods. By beginning *Marks* with a baptism, Bennett seems to be endorsing Locke's notion, which he invokes several times, each invocation imparting new tones and sounding new depths. Seventeen-year-old Margaret has spared her mother, Marjory, the disgrace of bringing an out-of-wedlock child into the family.

But Marjory is still chafing. Margaret's husband, a youth her own age, comes from common working-class stock, and their daughter has been named Kimberly, which irks Marjory. Eager to climb into the middle class, Marjory says of her new grand-daughter, "She's marked for life" (*OA* 87). The little girl will wear her name, which sounds as if it belongs to a place rather than a person, like a stigma. Being called Kimberly will seal off options for her, relegating her to a lower social rung than she might otherwise attain.

Marjory has other grievances. The canteen where she works has put her on short time. Earlier, her husband bolted the nest. And now that her daughter seems doomed to working-class squa-lor, Marjory has been trying to gentrify her son, Leslie, since only through him can she graze middle-class respectability. But he has dropped out of school, and, instead of looking for work near home, he is thinking of joining the army. The army has attracted him because it will put him beyond her reach. *Marks* is a Lawrencean story about a failed father and a blanketing mother. Marjory dotes so much on her fifteen-year-old son that he often listens to music on his headphones to shut out her endearments. She is forever making him uncomfortable. She calls him "lovely" (*OA* 89, 93, 111), touches and kisses him often, and embarrasses him by taking his arm in public. She also coaches him prior to a job interview. And because she believes him perfect (*OA* 111), she spends a great deal of time laundering his clothes, especially his white shirts, which she keeps fresh and spotless to reflect the glory she sees in him.

By calling Leslie perfect, she means that she sees him as her ideal companion—one she does not intend to share. Though she tells him how to act with girls, she drives away the only one he brings home, a fourteen-year-old named Lesley. The similarity between her son's name and that of his new girlfriend implies a closed circle that excludes Marjory. She has reason to be jealous. The two youngsters have more in common than she wants to admit. One of these areas of commonality is sex. To expunge the signs of Leslie and Lesley's afternoon rut, Marjory offers to wash his bed sheets. She will forgive Leslie anything. Unconcerned that he cannot spell or that he has never heard of Marlene Dietrich, she wants to create in him a partner to replace her absent husband. This nameless truant expresses what is wrong with the family and what will trouble it for years to come. Though that truant is living in Bristol, Marjory wants Les to tell any prospective employer that his father is dead. She is being unrealistic. She cannot rub out the marks the father has left not only on Les but also on her.

Lazy, ignorant, unmotivated Les will never become her business partner in the catering service she dreams of starting. He failed all his courses his last term in school, and, when not listening to rock music on his headphones, he is loitering on the sidelines of life; no actionist, he. He visits a skating rink not to skate but to watch, and he has no hobbies. "Spectating is not a hobby," an employment counselor tells him when he says that he enjoys watching hang gliders (*OA* 91). The counselor also labels him "a character with . . . no ideas . . . and no ambitions" (*OA* 92).

Nor will he rise from his doldrums so long as he is living with Marjory. But the knowledge that he can never attain full growth under her roof has made him uneasy. Prodded by guilt, he wants to demonstrate his love for her. He has the word *Mother* tattooed on his forearm. This loving gesture backfires. He had tried to tell her a story about a married couple, which she interrupted with the words, "I'm not interested in husbands and wives" (*OA* 111). She speaks the truth. Her attention has focused on mothers and sons. She refuses to date men her age. "I had a bellyful with a chap. Twice," she says, referring to the pregnancies that produced Margaret and Les (*OA* 93). The children's father, who could not even brew tea, also had a tattoo. Now Les has unconsciously followed his example. "It'll never come off. You're stuck with it. It's indelible," Marjory shrieks, insisting that the tattoo has killed her son's chances of getting a good job (*OA* 112). But most of her rage pivots on her statement, "You'll never be able to take your clothes off in front of a better class of people" (*OA* 113). The only women who would consider marrying him come from the same walk of life and speak the same lumpen dialect as the lowlifes she and Margaret both married. His tattoo has branded three generations of the family.

Marjory knows that upward social mobility will not come from her, a forty-three-year-old grandmother with only a part-time job who feels unwanted. Life has marked her, too. In the boldest, most aggressive image in all of Bennett, she hoists her skirt and yanks down her drawers to show Les her stretch marks from childbearing. These marks would repel any would-be lover, she believes. They may have even driven her husband away. She can live without sex, though. Despite the eroticism she has inscribed into her bond with Les, she has no sexual designs on him. In fact, she is grateful that she has found in him a man with whom she can share a sexless love. But she wants something richer and more vital for him, which she claims he has forfeited.

To shut out her rant, he puts on his headphones, which she rips off and smashes. Les is enraged. Calling her a "stupid cow" (*OA* 114), he hits her in the face. Their mutual rage cools quickly. Her first words after recovering from his blow, "You'll have me marked now," touch a nerve in him (*OA* 114). Rather than continuing to flail at her, he tells her to bathe the wound. Her response that he bathe his raw tattoo as well shows them making up. Like a married couple, they have quarreled and reconciled, each party yielding ground. They will probably walk the same dim, ambiguous course as Graham and his mother, Doris, of *A Chip in the Sugar.*

Les has been drained. The telefilm's short last scene shows him lying naked on a bed. Years have passed, and he is telling his story—the one that just appeared on screen—both to understand it and to wipe out the mark it has left on him. He is talking to another man, whose response shows that Les will wear his mark forever. "You've got a tattoo. Tattoos always turn me on," the man says (*OA* 114). He has not been listening to Les's story. But the story would not have moved him if he had listened. All he wants from Les is sex, which Les offers with resignation; being forced to look at his mother's stretch marks, or child scars, has killed in him the heterosexuality he displayed with Lesley. Like his tattooed father, he betrayed Marjory's love. The tattoo branded into him has bound him to her in ways he never knew existed. Mother and son are both marked or stained. Besides shocking and disgusting him, her stretch marks created in him great waves of pity. Having sex with another woman would dishonor the suffering the only woman who ever loved him endured for his sake. She has become for him an object of religious devotion, a motif enforced by the baptism service with which *Marks* began, by the ceremoniousness with which the tattooing is done (he says "Jesus" as the needle pierces his skin [*OA* 106]), and by the ancient-mariner-like rite of recounting his ordeal that Les keeps performing either to shake off Marjory's grip or to celebrate it.

Might he have become gay, anyway, even if Marjory's display of her stretch marks had not squelched his lust for women? With his father gone, he had no male role model in the home. And he certainly would not have wanted to emulate the tattoo artist, whose wife calls him "Dad," a frail alcoholic with tremors who operates from his grungy flat to avoid paying taxes. Les lacks outlets, all the more now that Margaret's marriage, having taken her out of the home, has left him one on one with Marjory. The strain caused by this new pairing manifests itself quickly. The day after the baptism, Marjory kisses him, marking his face with lipstick. "I've lipsticked you," she says, rubbing out the mark or pressing it into the skin (*OA* 94). Yet she continues to ogle him, and she practically ejects Lesley from the council flat she shares with Les. He might have well chosen to be gay to rule out the chance of intimacy with another Marjory. He may have also been protecting his autonomy. Nurturing impulses uniquely his might have been his only escape from her control.

This suggestion keys into the greatness of *Marks,* a work epical in its economy, simplicity, and drive. The deeper Bennett delves into the drab-looking lives of Marjory's family, the more profound and disturbing the work's dynamics become. *Marks* evokes mythical issues without chasing after myth. Maintaining a calm, balanced perspective while attaining this rare feat, it also

shows artistic eminence blossoming from the cash-driven, es-
tablishment-controlled medium that is television. Among its other
accomplishments, *Marks* shows how to beat the odds.

Conclusion

How will posterity judge Alan Bennett? As both actor and playwright, he satirizes vanity, hypocrisy, and stupidity. The keen ear that has helped his acting career has also sensitized him to both the weight and the tactile value of words. Thus his satire is often low key, graceful, and seductively skilled. His prose can glide along at a smooth, courteous pace reminiscent of the precision and buoyancy of J. B. Priestley or Noël Coward. Works ranging from the early *Forty Years On,* which Molly Panter-Downes called "a wild success,"[1] to the 1994 Academy Award nominee *Madness* include a wealth of funny, colorful scenes all the more remarkable for the apparent plainness of Bennett's prose. But this purveyor of witty satire will also violate decorum. Though a master of the light, perfectly timed glancing hit, he's no *petit-maître,* a French term for the English trait of perceiving one's limits and sticking to them. The subversive humor and sublime surreality of the Kafka plays and *The Old Crowd* disclose a Bennett far removed from the poised, pointed comedian of manners he is often taken to be. Bennett is one of the most self-plundering dramatists of our day. What has disguised his rage and torment is his preference for expressing himself without any sudden, jarring shifts in tone. His dialogue almost always sounds thoughtful, lucid, and either understated or ironic.

But this dab hand at "keeping it under" knows how to locate meaning beyond the lines being spoken (*WD* 15). Bennett's strategy of saying more than we hear from the actors also stems partly from the impression he gives of being a polymath. Though he will not let it hamper his plot structure or character development, the research that goes into his scripts is enormous. Chiropody drives the dramatic machinery of *A Private Function* just as heavy industry does that of *The Insurance Man* and art history that of *A Question of Attribution.* It is a proof of his artistry that his people do not look preassembled, cobbled up in advance of the plot rather than being allowed to reveal themselves in the course of it. Bennett's inner and outer selves commune with each other constantly and graciously, often imparting a melancholy that is either contained or voiced in jokes that divert our attention from it. His goal of writing scripts at once funny and sad raises him to heights occupied by very few. Though ironic and self-referential, he shuns obscure, deliberately playful rhetoric in his comments about art. Nor does he give a brutally unedited account of social problems.

But a set of ideas and issues does emerge from his work, allowing the individual scripts to build on each other and thus gain cumulative force. First, as is seen in the dashed hopes of Marjory in *Marks* and Midgley in *Intensive Care,* Bennett distrusts systems of thought. His work reflects an English preference for the specifics of experience over the abstractions of rational plans. It sets forth a banal world threatened by collapse and claustrophobia. Characters like the seven talking heads measure out their lives in teacups and memories of missed chances. They blend into their dingy surroundings even if, as in *Enjoy,* the surroundings change. By contrast, King George of *Madness* controls his surroundings when his wits return to him. He knows that putting on a good show for his followers sorts better with the disarray of the world than any blueprint theory of politics. Political decisions never rise from ideas about public policy or from first principles, anyway. The reason can only regulate what the passions dictate. Civic idealism and high-minded piety always fade into the everyday practice of government, which includes trade-offs, hidden agendas, and swindles.

Yet this sleaze sustains as it corrupts. Flawed as they are, public institutions structure life. In Bennett, ideas and purposes fuse with the way people enact them. If their enactment compromises and taints them, it also gives them substance. Thus those two constants of human activity, family and work, both corrode and preserve the people in *Rolling Home* and *Office Suite.* If the incarnation of an idea mars the idea's purity, it also endows it with blood and sinew, plucking it from the realm of abstraction, where it is useless, anyway. The translation of ideas into everyday experience can cause bitterness and heartbreak. Kafka's love-hate attitude toward fame in *Kafka's Dick* ties him, his father, and his literary executor Max Brod into knots that cannot even be unraveled in heaven. The blasting of Linda's hopes to marry a prince in *Enjoy* bogs her deeply in the moral quagmire she has been trying to escape. If the main figures of the three spy plays, *An Englishman Abroad, A Question of Attribution,* and *The Old Country,* were ever actuated by political justice, they have found Soviet communism so squalid and corrupt that they have had to cultivate a superfine gift for irony to fight off depression.

Their struggles are not conveyed as pieties or platitudes. Nor do they have the instructional smell of the classroom. Bennett's use of subtext to capture felt life makes the struggling

Judases Burgess, Blunt, and Hilary both funny and sad. Having learned how to laugh at themselves has helped this sad trio accept the punishment they know they deserve. This same self-detachment also makes them vulnerable and likable. Amalgams of virtue and nastiness, they evoke humanity at large. Their ambiguity implies absolution for their misdeeds, all the more so because, in extending charity to them, we are also absolving ourselves.

Such wonders of stage alchemy justify John Heilpern's calling Bennett in 1995 "one of England's national treasures."[2] Bennett has both the compassion and breadth of understanding to look at moral desolation and make audiences identify with it without mocking them. Those audiences can imagine themselves, like Muriel Carpenter of *Soldiering On,* forsaking their earthly goods rather than admitting to themselves that their children have cheated them into the poorhouse. Such identifications arise from compressed writing. Like the skits Bennett wrote for *Beyond the Fringe,* his best scripts have squeezed out all the fat. In them, he makes the writerly effort to fix a scene, omitting the extraneous and resisting the temptation to reach for the nearest phrase, to coast linguistically. This effort has brought him success on his own terms. Though he has earned a great deal of money with his plays, films, and television shows, he never seems actuated by the commercial impulse. His success comes, rather, from his originality, his complexity of thought and character, and his creative vigor.

Alan Bennett's writing conveys a sense of anger both controlled and transcended. He can describe ugliness without becoming its spokesperson. His instinct for wholeness also saves him from taking refuge in phony happy endings and conventional moralities. Any writer like him whose honesty and freshness of perception can point to a brighter future deserves serious attention.

Chapter 1: Tracking the Fringe

1. Alan Bennett, *Talking Heads* (London: BBC Books, 1988), 12. Subsequent references to this work will be noted parenthetically in the text as *TH.*

2. Hugh Davenport, "Hail the Foolish Virgins," [London] *Sunday Telegraph: Sunday Review,* 23 March 1997, 11.

3. Roger Wilmut, *From Fringe to Flying Circus: Celebrating a Unique Generation of Comedy 1960–1980* (London: Eyre Methuen, 1982), 11.

4. Peter Cook was BTF's first fatality. For Bennett's touching tribute to Cook as both colleague and friend, see Alan Bennett, "Alan Bennett Remembers Peter Cook," *London Review of Books* 17 (25 May 1995): 7; see also Lin Cook, ed., *Something Like Fire: Peter Cook Remembered* (London: Methuen, 1996), and Bevis Hiller, "Cook's Guided Tour, " *Spectator,* 2 November 1996, 42–44.

5. Wilmut, *From Fringe to Flying Circus,* 10.

6. Jack Kroll, "The Toast of London Town," *Newsweek,* 21 January 1991, 60; Ben Brantley, "Swimming in Irony," *New York Times Book Review,* 1 October 1995, 13.

7. Nicholas de Jongh, "Prime Time at Last: Alan Bennett," *Illustrated London News,* 25 December 1988, 42.

8. Matt Wolf, "Master of Eavesdropping and Empathy," *Times* (London), 20 January 1992, 10.

9. Michael Ratcliffe, "Franz Agonistes," *Observer,* 28 September 1986, 23; Brantley, "Swimming in Irony," 13; David Nokes, "The Body Politic," *TLS,* 16 December 1992, 18.

10. Christa Worthington, "Inside London: Bringing down the House," *Harper's Bazaar,* September 1989, 47; Alan Bennett, *Writing Home* (London: Faber and Faber, 1994), 177. Subsequent references to this work will be noted parenthetically in the text as *WH.*

11. John Russell Taylor, "The Bennett Plays," *Sight and Sound* 48 (spring 1979), 117.

12. Alan Bennett, *A Private Function: A Screenplay* (London: Faber and Faber, 1984), 96. Subsequent references will be noted parenthetically in the text as *PF*.

13. Harold Hobson, "Hobson's Choice," *Drama* 142 (1981), 29.

14. Alan Bennett, *Poetry in Motion* (London: Channel 4 Television), 58. Subsequent references to this work will be noted parenthetically in the text as *PM*.

15. Donald Lyons, "Theater: On the Superiority of European Methods," *New Criterion,* September 1992, 62.

16. Stephen Schiff, "Cultural Pursuits: The Poet of Embarrassment," *New Yorker,* 6 September 1993, 92.

17. Alan Bennett, Peter Cook, Jonathan Miller, and Dudley Moore, *The Complete* Beyond the Fringe, intro. Michael Frayne, ed. Roger Wilmut (London: Methuen, 1987), 123–25. Subsequent references to this work will be noted parenthetically in the text as *BTF*.

18. Alan Bennett, *Plays One:* Forty Years On, Getting On, Habeas Corpus, *and* Enjoy (London: Faber and Faber, 1997), 35. Subsequent references to this work will be noted parenthetically in the text as *Plays One.*

19. Alan Bennett, "Madness: The Movie," *London Review of Books* 17 (9 February 1995), 6.

20. J. B. Miller, "Far beyond the Fringe," *New York Times Magazine,* 3 March 1992, 36.

21. David Starkey, "Diary," *Spectator,* 3 February 1996, 7.

22. Alan Bennett, "Diary," *London Review of Books* 18 (4 January 1996), 25.

23. Wilmut, *From Fringe to Flying Circus,* 100.

24. Alan Bennett, introduction to *Objects of Affection and Other Plays for Television* (London: British Broadcasting Corporation, 1982),

26. Subsequent references to this work will be noted parenthetically in the text as *OA*.

25. Brantley, "Swimming in Irony," 13.

26. Alan Bennett, introduction to *Office Suite: Two One-Act Plays* (London: Faber and Faber, 1981), 8. Subsequent references to this work will be noted parenthetically in the text as *OS*.

Chapter 2: Ho, to Be in England

1. John Lahr, "The Theatre: Madjesty," *New Yorker,* 11 October 1993, 124.

2. Mollie Panter-Downes, "Letter from London," *New Yorker,* 14 November 1977, 197.

3. Frank Rich, "In London, a Writer's Three-Show Coup," *New York Times,* 3 March 1992, C17.

4. Alan Bennett, *Single Spies:* An Englishman Abroad *and* A Question of Attribution (London: Samuel French, 1991), 45. Subsequent references to this work will be noted parenthetically in the text as *SS*.

5. Patrick Skene Catling, "O Uncommon Alan Bennett," *Spectator* 260 (2 April 1988), 27.

6. Alan Bennett, introduction to Kenneth Grahame, *The Wind in the Willows* (London: Faber and Faber, 1991), xii.

7. Alan Bennett, *A Visit from Miss Prothero* (London: Samuel French, 1981), 10. Subsequent references to this work will be noted parenthetically in the text as *Visit*.

Chapter 3: Some Uses of History

1. Alan Bennett, *The Madness of George III* (London: Faber and Faber, 1991; rev. ed. 1995), xv. Subsequent references to this work will be noted parenthetically in the text as *MGIII*.

2. Irving Wardle, "Gielgud Is Starred as 'Forty Years On' Starts London Run," *New York Times,* 5 November 1968, 53.

3. Schiff, "Cultural Pursuits," 99.

4. Bernard Levin, *The Pendulum Years: Britain and the Sixties* (London: Jonathan Cape, 1970), 359.

5. Clive Barnes, "40 Years On," *New York Times,* 26 July 1969, 14.

6. Thomas Luddy, untitled review of *Enjoy, Library Journal,* 15 March 1981, 676.

7. Hobson, "Hobson's Choice," 29.

8. Lahr, "The Theatre," 124.

9. Bennett, "Madness: The Movie," 7.

10. Alan Bennett, *The Madness of King George* (London and New York: Faber and Faber, 1995), 60. Subsequent references to this work will be noted parenthetically in the text as *MKG.*

11. Bennett, "Madness: The Movie," 3.

12. Robert Brustein, *Dumbocracy in America: Studies in the Theatre of Guilt, 1987–1994* (Chicago: Ivan R. Dee, 1994), 26.

Chapter 4: Kafka and Other Office Drones

1. Alan Bennett, *Two Kafka Plays:* Kafka's Dick *and* The Insurance Man (London: Faber and Faber, 1987), 81. Subsequent references to this work will be noted parenthetically in the text as *Kafka.*

2. Alan Bennett, *The Writer in Disguise* (London: Faber and Faber, 1985), 118. Subsequent references to this work will be noted parenthetically in the text as *WD.*

3. Alan Bennett, *Green Forms* (London: Samuel French, 1981), 6. Subsequent references to this work will be noted parenthetically in the text as *GF.*

Chapter 5: Spies and Other Exiles

1. Erwin Panofsky, "Titian's *Allegory of Prudence:* A Postscript," in *Meaning in the Visual Arts* (1955; rpt. Phoenix ed. Chicago: University of Chicago Press, 1982), 149.

2. Frank Rich, "Bennett Breaks Ground in Britain as Aloof Meets Aloof in Spy Case," *New York Times,* 20 December 1988, C19.

3. Richard Hornby, untitled review of *Single Spies, Hudson Review* 43 (Winter 1990), 636.

4. Ibid.

5. Gilbert Cant, "The Puzzler," *Time,* 3 October 1977, 89.

6. Alan Bennett, *The Old Country* (London and Boston: Faber and Faber, 1978), 52. Subsequent references to this work will be noted parenthetically in the text as *OC.*

7. Harold Hobson, "Plays in Performance: Hobson's Choice," *Drama* 127 (winter 1977–78), 42.

8. Ibid., 41.

Chapter 6: On the Small Screen

1. Rich, "In London," C13.

2. Worthington, "Inside London," 48.

3. Steve Lohr, "The Verdigris of Life as Told (and Lived) by Alan Bennett," *New York Times,* 9 February 1989, C20.

4. Wolf, "Master of Eavesdropping and Empathy," 10.

5. Schiff, "Cultural Pursuits," 97.

6. Lohr, "Verdigris," C20.

7. Sheridan Morley, "I, Coriolanus," *Spectator,* 22 June 1996, 42.

8. Nicholas Wapshott, "Alan Bennett: Quite Often Managing to Make Himself Wince," *Times* (London), 27 November 1978, 7.

9. Taylor, "The Bennett Plays," 117, 118.

10. Morley, "I, Coriolanus," 42.

Conclusion

1. Mollie Panter-Downes, "Letter from London," *New Yorker,* 14 December 1968, 207.

2. John Heilpern, "Empires for the Stage," photographs by Snowdon, *Vanity Fair* 423 (November 1995), 196.

BIBLIOGRAPHY

Works by Alan Bennett (Chronological)

The Old Country. London and Boston: Faber and Faber, 1978.

Green Forms (from *Office Suite*). London: Samuel French, 1981.

Office Suite: Two One-Act Plays. London: Faber and Faber, 1981.

A Visit from Miss Prothero (from *Office Suite*). London: Samuel French, 1981.

Objects of Affection and Other Plays for Television. London: British Broadcasting Corporation, 1982.

A Woman of No Importance. London: Samuel French, 1982.

A Private Function: A Screenplay. London: Faber and Faber, 1984.

The Writer in Disguise. London: Faber and Faber, 1985.

Two Kafka Plays: Kafka's Dick *and* The Insurance Man. London: Faber and Faber, 1987.

Talking Heads. London: BBC Books, 1988; Jersey City, N.J.: Parkwest, 1992.

Poetry in Motion. London: Channel 4 Television, 1990.

The Madness of George III. London and Boston: Faber and Faber, 1991; rev. ed. 1995.

Single Spies: An Englishman Abroad *and* A Question of Attribution. London: Samuel French, 1991.

Writing Home. London: Faber and Faber, 1994; New York: Random House, 1995.

The Madness of King George. London and Boston: Faber and Faber, 1995.

Plays One: Forty Years On, Getting On, Habeas Corpus, *and* Enjoy. London: Faber and Faber, 1997.

Adaptations by Alan Bennett

Grahame, Kenneth. *The Wind in the Willows.* London: Faber and Faber, 1991.

Orton, Joe. *Prick up Your Ears.* London: Faber and Faber, 1987.

BIBLIOGRAPHY

Collaboration

Bennett, Alan, Peter Cook, Jonathan Miller, and Dudley Moore. *The Complete* Beyond the Fringe. Introd. Michael Frayne. Ed. Roger Wilmut. London: Methuen, 1987.

Fiction

Bennett, Alan. *The Clothes They Stood Up In.* London: Profile Books, 1998.

Selected Articles by Alan Bennett (Chronological)

"Where I Was in 1993." *London Review of Books* 15 (16 December 1993): 3, 5, 6.
"Madness: The Movie." *London Review of Books* 17 (9 February 1995): 3, 6, 7.
"Alan Bennett Remembers Peter Cook." *London Review of Books* 17 (25 May 1995): 7.
"Diary." *London Review of Books* 18 (4 January 1996): 24–25.

Criticism and Commentary

Anderson, Lindsay, "An Introduction," in Bennett, *The Writer in Disguise,* 161–75. Discusses his attempt to develop the "epical qualities" of *The Old Crowd.*
Barnes, Clive. "40 Years On." *New York Times,* 26 July 1969, 14. Scathes the play for its alleged "pretentiousness and ineptness."
———. "A Parade of Wit for 'Habeas Corpus.'" *New York Times,* 26 November 1975, 12. Expresses discomfort with the play's excessive carnality and sexuality.

BIBLIOGRAPHY

Brantley, Ben. "Swimming in Irony." *New York Times Book Review,* 1 October 1995, 13–14. A sound, insightful discussion of Bennett's subtlety and indirection.

Brustein, Robert. *Dumbocracy in America: Studies in the Theatre of Guilt, 1987–1994.* Chicago: Ivan R. Dee, 1994. Argues that *Madness of George III* establishes Bennett's importance as an "epic playwright."

————. *Seasons of Discontent: Dramatic Opinions, 1959–1965.* New York: Simon and Schuster, 1965. Praises *Beyond the Fringe* for its healthy, liberating attitudes.

Campbell, Donald. Untitled review of four works by Alan Bennett. *British Book News,* June 1985, 368. Finds both merits and flaws (*Getting On* is "seriously over-written") in Bennett.

Cant, Gilbert. "The Puzzler." *Time,* 3 October 1977, 89. Discusses the importance of English social values and traditions in *The Old Country.*

Catling, Patrick Skene. "O Uncommon Alan Bennett." *Spectator* 260 (2 April 1988): 27–28. Commends Bennett's ability to transform the ordinary into the "significantly poetic."

Davenport, Hugh, "Hail the Foolish Virgins." [London] *Sunday Telegraph: Sunday Review,* 23 March 1997, 11. Studies Bennett's adaptations of biblical tales for television.

de Jongh, Nicholas. "Prime Time at Last: Alan Bennett." *Illustrated London News,* 25 December 1988, 41–42. Argues that Bennett has achieved greater artistic heights than any of his former colleagues from *Beyond the Fringe.*

de Lacy, Justine. "Portrait of a 'Cambridge Spy.'" *New York Times,* 28 October 1984, sec. 2, p. 28. Discusses the importance of exile and betrayal in Bennett's plays.

Heilpern, John. "Empires for the Stage." Photographs by Snowdon. *Vanity Fair* 423 (November 1995): 189–225. Praises Bennett ("one of England's national treasures") in a long photographic essay on current British theater.

Hobson, Harold. "Hobson's Choice." *Drama* [London: British Theatre Association] 142 (1981): 27–30. Shows how the Bennett of *Enjoy* mixes different theatrical techniques, like naturalism and surrealism, to attack the bureaucracy of the day.

———. "Plays in Performance: Hobson's Choice." *Drama* [London: British Theatre Association] 127 (Winter 1977–78): 39–44. Finds beauty and elegance in the structure of *The Old Country.*

Hornby, Richard. Untitled review of *Single Spies. Hudson Review* 43 (winter 1990): 629–36. Praises Bennett's characterization of Queen Elizabeth II in *A Question of Attribution.*

Kakutani. Michiko. "Books of the Times: Feet Dry and No Egg on His Face." *New York Times,* 26 September 1995, C14. Claims that dislocation in Bennett is modulated by pluck and a sense of fun.

Kroll, Jack. "The Toast of London Town." *Newsweek,* 21 January 1991, 60. Hails Bennett as the most talented of the foursome who comprised *Beyond the Fringe.*

Lahr, John. "The Theatre: Madjesty." *New Yorker,* 11 October 1993, 124–26. Cites Bennett's masterful use of irony in his portrayals of English society.

Levin, Bernard. *The Pendulum Years: Britain and the Sixties.* London: Jonathan Cape, 1970. Finds in the "widely misunderstood and dismissed" *Forty Years On* a brilliant portrayal of the challenges posed by both the future and the past.

Lohr, Steve. "The Verdigris of Life as Told (and Lived) by Alan Bennett." *New York Times,* 9 February 1989, C17, 20. Discusses the layered, multileveled techniques that give rise to the *Talking Heads* monologues.

Luddy, Thomas. Untitled review of *Enjoy. Library Journal,* 15 March 1981, 676. Recommends this "most successful play."

BIBLIOGRAPHY

Lyons, Donald. "Theater: On the Superiority of European Methods." *New Criterion* [New York], 11 (September 1992): 59–63. Argues well that Bennett is a minimalist or miniaturist.

Mallet, Gina. Untitled review of *Habeas Corpus. Time,* 8 December 1975, 91. Attacks *Habeas Corpus* as "a sloppy farce" that suffers from being "entirely predictable and unabashedly vulgar."

Miller, J. B. "Far beyond the Fringe." *New York Times Magazine,* 3 March 1992, 36, 37, 82, 90–91. Claims that *Beyond the Fringe* influenced the Beatles, Monty Python, and "almost every BBC situation comedy of the last decade."

Morley, Sheridan. "I, Coriolanus." *Spectator,* 22 June 1996, 41–42. Praises the adaptability of the written-for-TV *Talking Heads* series to the stage.

Museum of Television and Radio Broadcasting (New York). "The BBC Seminar." 25 November 1986 (Museum of Television and Radio Broadcasting, 25 West 52nd Street, New York, NY 10019). Justifies the need for irony to portray complex and even contradictory emotions on the stage.

Nokes, David. "The Body Politic." *TLS,* 16 December 1992, 18. Claims that Bennett's popularity follows from his outstanding skill: "he is probably our greatest living dramatist."

Panofsky, Erwin. "Titian's *Allegory of Prudence:* A Postscript." In *Meaning in the Visual Arts*, 146–68. 1955; rpt. Phoenix ed. Chicago: University of Chicago Press, 1982. The three (or five) faces in Titian's painting symbolize different states of being, all of which lend resonance to Bennett's satire on spying in *A Question of Attribution*.

Panter-Downes, Mollie. "Letter from London." *New Yorker,* 14 December 1968, 202–8. Time shifting, historical sense, and humor make *Forty Years On* a "wild success."

BIBLIOGRAPHY

————. "Letter from London." *New Yorker,* 14 November 1977, 194–97. Traces with accuracy and depth the theme of failure in several Bennett plays.

Peter, John. "Drama." *Sunday Times: Culture,* 9 June 1996, 16–17. Recommends *Habeas Corpus* as "the wisest and funniest show in London."

Ratcliffe, Michael. "Franz Agonistes." *Observer,* 28 September 1986, 23. Judging from *Kafka's Dick,* Bennett is "one of the funniest and most fastidious writers working in England today."

Rich, Frank. "Bennett Breaks Ground in Britain as Aloof Meets Aloof in Spy Case." *New York Times*, 20 December 1988, C19–20. Sees *A Question of Attribution* as aflame with subtext and "subversive innuendo."

————. "In London, a Writer's Three-Show Coup." *New York Times,* 3 March 1992, C13, 17. Finds value in the compassion with which dislocation, loneliness, and self-deception are presented in *Talking Heads.*

Schiff, Stephen. "Cultural Pursuits: The Poet of Embarrassment." *New Yorker,* 6 September 1993, 92–101. Discusses the tension between appearance and reality in Bennett.

Starkey, David. "Diary." *Spectator,* 3 February 1996, 7. Commends Bennett's power to invoke England's industrial North in plays.

Taylor, John Russell. "The Bennett Plays." *Sight and Sound* 48 (spring 1979): 116–18. Admires the technical ingenuity of *The Old Crowd* but dismisses it as "arid and sterile."

Turner, D[aphne] E. *Alan Bennett: In a Manner of Speaking.* London: Faber and Faber, 1997. A wise look at the development of Bennett's artistic sensibilities; particularly helpful with Bennett's unpublished television plays.

Wapshott, Nicholas. "Alan Bennett: Quite Often Managing to Make Himself Wince." *Times* (London), 27 November 1978, 7. Sees strength flowing into the Bennett scripts from sources like self-knowledge, a keen eye, and a good heart.

Wardle, Irving. "Gielgud Is Starred as '40 Years On' Starts London Run." *New York Times,* 5 November 1968, 53. Argues that setting, pageant, and myth create in *Forty Years On* a powerful "image of Britain at the crossroads."

Wilmut, Roger. *From Fringe to Flying Circus: Celebrating a Unique Generation of Comedy 1960–1980.* London: Eyre Methuen, 1982. Surveys developments in British comedy.

Wolf, Matt. "Master of Eavesdropping and Empathy." *Times* [London], 20 January 1992, 10. Contrasts Bennett's modesty with his outstanding success as a writer.

Worthington, Christa. "Inside London: Bringing down the House." *Harper's Bazaar,* September 1989, 46–48. Marvels at the clash between Bennett's understatedness and the great stature he has gained on the British stage.

INDEX

INDEX

INDEX

253

INDEX

Moore, Dudley, 2, 3
More, Kenneth, 10
Morley, Sheridan, 198, 217
Mountbatten, Philip: wedding with Princess Elizabeth, 49
Mowbray, Michael, 49
Murdoch, Iris, *The Sandcastle,* 41

New Yorker, 68
Newman, Cardinal John Henry, 102
Nicholson, Harold, 36
Nokes, David, 4

Observer (London), 212
Olivier, Lawrence, 4
Orton, Joe, 86
Osborne, John, 3

Pankovsky, Erwin, 151–52
Panter-Downes, Mollie, 21, 227
Philby, Kim, 134, 148, 150
Pinter, Harold, 30–31
Pirandello, Luigi, 149; *Each in His Own Way,* 42; *Henry IV,* 37, 81
Plato, 78
Plowright, Joan, 3, 55
Polanski, Roman, *Tess,* 196
Postlethwaite, Pete, 52, 135
Priestley, J. B., 227
Proust, Marcel, 179
Puccini, Giacomo, *Madame Butterfly,* 112

Ratcliffe, Michael, 4
Rattigan, Terence, 20, 217

INDEX